'*Bully Blocking* contains many imaginative suggestions for parents and children on how to cope with the problem of being victimised by their peers at school.'

Ken Rigby, Adjunct Professor, University of South Australia,
author of Bullying in Schools and What to Do About It

'Evelyn Field's thoughtful and beautifully written book is both timely and needed, providing young people and their carers with a variety of skills, knowledge and strategies to counter the problem of bullying and teasing. The illustrations and activity pages ensure the user-friendliness of the book for young people. *Bully Blocking* is a "must read" for parents who want to give their children the gift of a range of social and emotional competencies to help them traverse the sometimes rocky terrain of the schoolyard and beyond.'

Associate Professor Michael Carr-Gregg, PhD MAPS,
author of Surviving Year 12 and co-author of Adolescence

'Evelyn Field has drawn on her vast clinical experience over many years of working with children, their families and teachers to write a superb book about all aspects of bullying. Beginning with descriptions of different types of bullying, Field goes on to list the manifestations and consequences of bullying, and devotes the rest of the book to information and practical exercises as to what parents, teachers (and children, too) can do. It is written in a style that is interesting, very practical and easy to read. *Bully Blocking* is an invaluable resource for children, parents, teachers and all professionals working with children who are aware of the often devastating consequences of bullying that is allowed to go unchecked.'

Professor Frank Oberklaid,
Director, Centre for Community Child Health,
Royal Children's Hospital Melbourne

'Parents of today's children see no place for bullying. They also are seeking a strong partnership with schools to ensure all children are happy and safe at school. In *Bully Blocking*, Evelyn Field provides parents with a most practical and easy-to-read road map into the future without bullying. Parents who unfold Evelyn's road map will find support and confidence to make that journey successful for their children and their school communities.'

Duncan McInnes, Executive Officer,
NSW Parents Council Inc.

'This is a book packed with practical ideas for parents and children to use in understanding and addressing bullying. Evelyn writes with confidence and clarity, and I like her light-hearted presentation. Few of the books available on bullying target both the parent and the child readership – *Bully Blocking* does. It is easy to read, and the extensive information is presented in an attractive format.'

Dr Valerie Besag, Consultant Educational Psychologist,
author of Understanding Girls' Friendships, Fights and Feuds:
A Practical Approach to Girls' Bullying

D0905314

Bully Blocking

of related interest

Asperger Syndrome and Bullying
Strategies and Solutions
Nick Dubin
Foreword by Michael John Carley
ISBN 978 1 84310 846 7

Being Bullied
Strategies and Solutions for People with Asperger's Syndrome
Nick Dubin
(DVD)
ISBN 978 1 84310 843 6

New Perspectives on Bullying
Ken Rigby
ISBN 978 1 85302 872 4

Listening to Young People in School
Youth Work and Counselling
Nick Luxmoore
ISBN 978 1 85302 909 7

Working with Anger and Young People
Nick Luxmoore
ISBN 978 1 84310 466 7

Nurture Groups in School and at Home
Connecting with Children with Social, Emotional and Behavioural Difficulties
Paul Cooper and Yonca Tiknaz
ISBN 978 1 84310 528 2

Bully Blocking

Six Secrets to Help Children Deal with Teasing and Bullying

Revised Edition

Evelyn M. Field

Jessica Kingsley Publishers
London and Philadelphia

This work was originally published in Australia and New Zealand as *Bully Blocking:*
Six secrets to help children deal with teasing and bullying, by Finch Publishing Pty Limited, Sydney, in 2007 and is a
revised edition of *Bullybusting: How to help children deal with teasing and bullying*, published by Finch Publishing in 1999.

This edition published in the United Kingdom in 2007
by Jessica Kingsley Publishers
116 Pentonville Road
London N1 9JB, UK
and
400 Market Street, Suite 400
Philadelphia, PA 19106, USA

www.jkp.com

Library of Congress Cataloging in Publication Data

Field, Evelyn M.
    [Bully busting]
    Bully blocking : six secrets to help children deal with teasing and bullying / Evelyn M. Field.
       p. cm.
    Originally published: Bully busting. Sydney : Finch Pub., c1999.
    Includes bibliographical references and index.
    ISBN 978-1-84310-554-1 (pb : alk. paper) 1. Bullying. 2. Bullying—Prevention. 3. Teasing. 4. Teasing—Prevention. 5.
Children—Life skills guides. I. Title.
    BF637.B85F54 2007
    302.3—dc22

                                                                            2007004825

British Library Cataloguing in Publication Data
A CIP catalogue record for this book is available from the British Library

ISBN 978 184310 554 1

Printed and bound in the United States by
Thomson-Shore, Inc.

Notes The 'Authors' notes' section at the back of this book contains useful additional information and references to quoted material in the text. Each reference is linked to the text by its relevant page number and an identifying line entry.

Disclaimers While every care has been taken in researching and compiling the information in this book, it is in no way intended to replace professional legal advice and counselling. Readers are encouraged to seek such help as they deem necessary. The authors and publisher specifically disclaim any liability arising from the application of information in this book.

TM The term *Bully Blocking* has been trademarked by Evelyn Field.

Confidentiality Most stories in this book are an extract or a collage of several actual cases. Where relevant, permission has been obtained from the family concerned. Any similarity to reality is simply due to the commonality of many situations.

Warning This book has been designed to assist targets, bullies and peers, but it is not a therapy book. If the child is very depressed, anxious, traumatised or extremely abusive – or if you feel stuck and powerless – then the publisher and author encourage you to consult a skilled mental health professional.

*To Miriam, my beautiful first child, who has gone
to another universe but gave me the model 'the Secrets of
Relating'; and to my children, Rebecca and David,
who gave me the strength and courage to develop it.*

*To my sister, Vivienne, my brother-in-law, Ruben, and my
mother, Marianne, my daughter-in-law, Anna, my very special
family and my friends for their love, support and understanding.*

*I would also like to dedicate this book to my special friend,
Barbara Levy, who blossomed from a shy bud into a beautiful,
beloved rose.*

*Thank you to Bufy and Harry, my two papillions, for keeping
me company while I wrote this new version and for coaching me
in basic social survival skills.*

'Eternal vigilance is the price of liberty.'
Thomas Jefferson

'The only thing necessary for evil to triumph
is for good men to do nothing.'
Edmund Burke

Contents

Introduction 9

Part One — Understanding Bullying 13

  1.   Bullying – an overview 15

  2.   Bullies and targets 27

  3.   What causes bullying? 37

  4.   The damage done 47

Part Two — Taking Action 57

  5.   First, transform your child's attitudes 59

  6.   How parents can help 76

  7.   What schools can do 108

Part Three — The Six Secrets of Relating   127

8. Regulate your feelings – Secret 1   131

9. Understand why you are bullied or a bully
    – Secret 2   148

10. Build your self-esteem – Secret 3   164

11. Become a confident communicator – Secret 4   180

12. Create your own 'power pack' – Secret 5   201

13. Develop a support network – Secret 6   223

Teachers' supplement   235

Author's notes   238

Acknowledgements   243

Resources   246

Index   249

Introduction

Bully Blocking is designed to help children and their parents and teachers deal with bullies of all shapes, sizes and disguises. It can also assist families whose children bully occasionally or regularly. It is a self-help book, with practical activities that any child or adult can translate into action. It shows children who have been targets of bullying how to empower themselves, and it shows children who bully how to use their power with empathy and respect. It provides parents with simple, clear, practical ideas for helping their children stop being a target or a bully. Families can find the necessary information and guidance to change painful school situations into successful social experiences.

Bully Blocking is based on the experience I have gained during over 30 years as a school-based psychologist and in private practice, assisting children, parents and their teachers. Many children have shared their own successful bully-blocking strategies with me. I have also received inspiration and feedback from my presentations at workshops, conferences and seminars in Australia, New Zealand, the US, Israel, Vietnam, Belgium, Spain and Norway. And since the advent of my website, I have received worldwide feedback.

The confidence to develop my ideas and write this book originally came from the strong support I received from the media. Many years ago, former journalist Terry Willessee challenged me to respond to a tease on television. 'You are fat,' he said. To show how effective humour can be in dealing with teasing and bullying, my reply was, 'Don't be ridiculous, I'm enormous!'

This revised and updated book has been shaped by the changes in current research, especially the impact that families can have on their children's target or bullying behaviours, as well as the limited power of most schools to reduce bullying and implement a truly whole-school approach. Many parents have to teach their children how to cope with bullying in an imperfect educational system. This book has also been influenced by my own recent personal and professional experiences with workplace bullying. This demonstrates the need for children to develop effective social survival skills, which will be useful anywhere, especially if they encounter workplace bullying later on.

Most children I meet in my practice are targets of bullying: they feel powerless, hopeless, scared, angry and depressed. They can't learn new skills with the same ease that others do. Like any other trauma victim, they need empathy, patience and simple activities to help them move forward. It takes time and encouragement for both targets and bullies to transform their attitudes, change their behaviours, and empower themselves.

The six secrets of 'bully blocking' – 'The Secrets of Relating' – form the unique core of the book. I have created this programme as a generic, circular model. By constantly practising different aspects of the model, any child with social challenges will improve their self-protective, assertive and social survival skills. The techniques in the six secrets will help parents work out with their children what they can do if the children are teased, excluded, electronically or physically bullied, or if they bully others. Parents can use some exercises to renovate their own role modelling to help their child. They play an essential role in encouraging their child to practise effective activities, change and take action.

Some exercises appear incredibly simple, like maintaining eye contact. But this simplicity is deceptive: these concepts and exercises have been used successfully with depressed and traumatised people. Some exercises work for everyone; others offer options, such as a range of retorts and ways to deal with exclusion. Their effectiveness depends upon the child's age, abilities and each individual situation. Obtain feedback from others, then apply your intuition and common sense to help your child discover what he or she feels comfortable doing. Encourage them to be flexible, and select from the options, like a recipe book. A few of these options may feel comfortable instantly, others may require practice, and perhaps some won't feel right at all. Although nothing in this book is aggressive or destructive, be aware that some techniques may not be suitable for your child or his or her school. You may find that your child can reduce the bullying or teasing simply by reading, discussing, laughing, visualising, planning or practising some of the ideas. Once children release their fears and frustrations, transform their attitudes, adopt new assertive behaviours and friendship skills, the bullying should cease.

The new chapter on what schools can do (Chapter 7) is based upon my work with primary and secondary schools. It reflects the need for schools to acknowledge bullying and take action to protect all concerned; it provides a simple, concise outline for dealing with bullying. There is also a 'Teachers' supplement' for those who would like to use some of the book's many activities and exercises in the classroom. Teachers can apply some activities individually, or integrate them into the curriculum. Health professionals and others with limited resources to survey the current literature can also benefit from the book's practical skills and simple overview. I have included a reading list and additional notes at the back of the book for parents, counsellors, psychologists, social workers, nurses, psychiatrists, police and others working with young people.

Life is not always easy, but you *can* teach a child how to develop social and emotional resilience by providing him or her with simple social survival skills to protect him- or herself and deal with difficult, stressful encounters. Learning these social survival skills is essential for all children. Bullies also have a right to enjoy a normal social life: they need to learn how to change their behaviours so that they feel socially secure and valued.

Many of the stories and ideas included here are designed to bring *a smile* to the child's face. Once children can smile, they are better equipped to change their attitude and, consequently, what they do. When they have mastered the skills presented in this book, they can then learn how to apply them in other areas of their lives. This is a real bonus. Then, you and your family can watch shy, scared, frustrated, abusive or powerless youngsters become happier people who enjoy life.

Evelyn M. Field, FAPS, ASM

A note on language: In the interests of gender fairness, the use of 'he' and 'she' alternates after each major heading within chapters when the text is general and does not apply to a specific child or gender.

PART ONE

UNDERSTANDING BULLYING

1

Bullying – an overview

What kids say about bullies

'Adam is always calling people who are littler than him names.'

'Darren always calls you names and he hits you when you walk past. Kids are sick of him.'

'Jason teases me just because I'm different and he makes me upset.'

'Kim spreads lies about me by email every week.'

'I hate the fact that I don't know who's spreading nasty gossip about me in the chat group or who is sending texts [text messages] to my phone.'

'I walked around the corner and Jeff kicked me for no reason.'

'Sally punches, pushes and pinches me and pulls my hair.'

'Sometimes Adrian criticises me at sport and upsets me.'

'I'm worried about getting into a fight with Debbie before camp because she would turn everyone against me, but I still want to be in her cabin.'

'Mike said, "I'm going to get you after school".'

'It's cool to bully at our school.'

'Bullies can smell you a mile away.'

About bullying

Every year, many parents pass on a simple, sound instruction to their child: 'If you are nice to people, they will be nice to you.' But some children get the wrong idea. They don't know how to be nice effectively – they are nice but vulnerable, or they seem polite but are more concerned with how they feel or appear than with showing genuine care for others. Naturally, other children may sense this lack of interest, and bully them in retaliation.

Children respect children who are friendly and real, who say what they think and feel, who stand up for themselves. But even if a child is friendly and real, some others may still bully him or her. The result is that many children will arrive at school each day feeling scared, frustrated and powerless. And sadly, the impact of bullying boomerangs back on the bully, who also suffers.

Bullying in school has always existed, and many regard it as a 'part of life'. But our community has received a wake-up call in the form of the number of suicides, violent attacks and murders that bullying creates. Bullying is a symptom of a dysfunctional social system.

While the focus of this book is students bullying students, bullying also occurs between students, teachers, parents and the school community, creating combinations such as parents bullying teachers, teachers bullying students, and so on.

Here are a few facts about bullying:

- Bullying involves psychological, emotional, social or physical abuse.

- The crucial feature is perception: the target feels powerless.

- The critical issue is the extent of the damage done to the target.

- About one in five students is bullied regularly, and around one in five bully regularly.

- A bully may or may not intend to hurt.

Where does bullying occur?

- In any school, poor or wealthy, private or state, co-educational or single-sex, small or large, religious or non-religious, conservative, traditional or progressive, day or boarding schools.

- At school: in the classroom, the playground, canteen, toilets, lockers, sporting facilities, change rooms, isolated corridors, school camp.

- Outside school: travelling to and from school, at after-school care programmes, playgrounds, shopping centres, discos.

- In cyberspace: text messages, emails, Internet chat rooms and websites, bulletin boards, digital photographs.

The bullying continuum

This bullying continuum illustrates the progressive escalation from harmless banter to bullying and criminal behaviours.

Social banter

Hurtful teasing

Mean, subtle body language

Aggressive physical behaviours, e.g. pushing, shoving, kicking

Malicious gossip, e.g. online bullying, chat rooms

Sexual, gender, racist, religious harassment

Social exclusion – in person, electronic

Mobbing

Hazing

Extortion/bribery

Phone, cyber abuse

Damage to property

Physical violence

Use of weapons

Criminal act

Murder

Types of bullying

There are four main types of bullying: teasing, exclusion, physical bullying and harassment.

1. Teasing

Teasing is verbal violence. It is the most dangerous and long-lasting form of bullying. The most common forms of teasing are related to appearance, sexuality and social approval. A word that is regarded as normal in one school (or country) may be really bad in another. Although the words vary, it is the intent, the audience and the social context that harm the target. The tease hurts because of the bully's mean, sarcastic manner, tone, facial expression and regular repetition. The main types of teasing are:

- name-calling

- harassing, yelling, insulting or nagging

- verbal demands or threats

- making a noise as the target walks past, and

- phone abuse, nasty notes, Internet, email, SMS texting and other electronic forms.

2. Exclusion

'Exclusion' or 'relational' bullying is based on social manipulation, and can be expressed openly – 'You can't sit with us' – as well as involving indirect, subtle, secret behaviours or nonverbal body language by the bully and others. A bully can manipulate the group without his direct involvement, by using the social structure to attack the target. The goal of exclusion is to create a group identity that becomes a powerful control mechanism. Each group member knows that if he tries to protect the target, he may be next. When a bully is devious, the teacher's presence is irrelevant – a raised eyebrow may be enough to frighten a target. Sadly, many teachers miss indirect aggression and thus deny its presence. Exclusion includes:

- pretending to be friendly to the target and then sporadically turning against him

- as the target approaches, the group giving him 'the silent treatment' and turning their backs

- the bully saying something to the target and walking off before he can reply

- pointing, staring, sniggering, laughing, making faces, mimicking, or whispering with others while looking at the target

- threatening poses, menacing gestures, 'the look'

- excluding the child from the peer group, conversation, planned activities or games

- not sharing a seat while pretending to save it for someone else

- malicious gossip and rumours designed to make other children denigrate the target, e.g. exposing his secrets to others, and

- extortion and threats, e.g. 'I won't be your friend if you don't buy me a snack', 'You won't come to my party if you don't give me your project to copy'.

3. Physical

Physical bullying involves regularly attacking someone who is weaker. It can be directly aggressive, such as hitting, kicking and spitting; or indirect, such as by gesture, suggestion, stalking, and defacing or hiding property. It can include grabbing the target by his clothing and tearing it or being involved in fights in which he is defenceless. It includes:

- pushing, shoving, kicking, pinching, punching, bumping, knocking, hair-pulling, physical restraint, tripping up, and the use of weapons

- stealing books, lunch or other possessions from a desk or locker

- throwing someone's belongings around the classroom

- interfering with or damaging a child's clothes, belongings in his desk, locker or elsewhere, e.g. pushed over, broken or hidden

- taking away the chair as a child is about to sit on it

- locking him in a room or cupboard, putting his head in a toilet

- flicking water at the child from the tap, flicking bits of paper or rubber bands, and

- sabotaging homework or computer studies.

4. Harassment

Harassment generally involves repeated, annoying questions, statements or attacks about sexual, gender, racial, religious or nationality issues. It includes:

- subjecting a child to any sexual gestures, interference, acts of physical intimacy and assaults via touching, grabbing or pinching, e.g. fondling a girl's breasts, touching a child's bottom or other private parts, flicking a girl's skirt, urinating at someone

- pulling the target's underpants down in front of other students

- looking under the toilet door

- making direct or indirect comments about a child's sexuality: 'You're gay', 'You're a homo/lesbian', 'You're a girl' (to a boy)

- using intimidating language, e.g. 'Fuck off', 'Go fuck your mother', 'Your mother is a slut', 'Go back to where you came from'

- making unwelcome sexual advances or requests, and

- stalking inside or outside the school.

Gender differences in bullying

- Boys and girls bully equally and both can be targets. Boys bully boys and girls. Girls usually bully other girls, but can also bully boys.

- Boys often use bullying tactics to make a reputation and girls often do so to protect their reputation.

- Boys tend to be hunters who belong to large, hierarchical tribes. They typically bully openly and prefer physical bullying. They focus upon individual achievement and action, supported by their physical prowess. They are less interested in teasing, exclusion and indirect bullying.

- Girls tend to be gatherers who socialise in smaller, intimate friendship groups. They typically prefer teasing or indirect, less physical bullying. They use verbal denigration, malicious gossip and exclusion as powerful weapons to manage, manipulate and protect their small group friendships.

- Girls tend to be 'bitchy' or passive-aggressive, while boys tend to be 'macho' or aggressive. While males deny bullying, females hope others will intuitively sense it.

- Bullies (and targets) of both sexes usually have poorly-developed assertive communication skills.

The bullying game

Bullying is a game where some children systematically abuse their power. Bullies can go on a shopping spree at the beginning of every year looking for suitable targets. The bullying game may occur over a period of time, sometimes years, with the same players, or the target may confront a series of bullies. Some children are always targeted and others are serial bullies. Some children switch from target to bully and then back again depending on the situation. The bully may be nice in class but exclude in the playground. The bully may be a friend or someone within the target's social group. The group can invite the target to join them, alienate her from decent friends, and then reject the target. In some cases neither player enjoys this heartless game. They don't know how to change, stop or remove themselves. Some don't realise that they are bullying. Regardless of conscious or unconscious intent, they can do great harm and can cause significant damage.

In fact, the target can alter the rules of the game to stop getting hurt. She can remove herself, become detached, obtain assistance or use other techniques to block the bullying. Say to your child, 'Pretend the family has won a wonderful trip overseas. You will be absent from school for four weeks. Who will the bully hurt instead?' Guess what? Most children know who's next because they know who else is vulnerable. *They know how the game works.*

So how *does* it work? Let's look at the rules.

Rule 1: Bullies need a reaction

Most people know that you don't show your fear or anger to a horse or dog because it will react. The same applies to dealing with bullies. You may think it's amazing that bullies know whom to bully. But they don't. Research has shown that some pick on nearly everyone at the beginning of a year, until someone reacts. Perhaps bullies smell fear or anger like animals do and react out of self-protection. However, the target's behaviours inform the bully that she qualifies as a good target.

Bullies, like Customs officials, respond to the target's change in facial expression, body language, voice and actions following the initial attack. If the target remains neutral in a blank, trance-like, spaced-out state, the bully's power dissipates. But when a child reacts, her distress escalates the game and empowers the bully. Any sign of fear or anger from a target makes a bully happy. The target makes it easy for a bully to release frustrations, enhance her social status and make her day. The bully knows that the target can't protect herself – this reinforces the bully, who can automatically pick on the child without needing to search for a new target every day.

Ask your child, 'What do you say or do when she bullies you?' Look for common reactions, like, 'I do nothing, walk away or I say something back'. Ask what happens if she refuses to play the bully's game! Then coach her to use some assertive techniques (see Chapter 11).

Parents and kids activity

Rule 2: Play the game

Siblings banter and bully frequently. Later on, they make up under parental guidance or family cohesion. They know when they can play the game and when they can't. Similarly, there seems to be an odd ongoing connection or collusion between some bullies and their targets. Dr Debra Pepler has found an ongoing relationship between the bully and the target. The target rewards the aggressive bully by being submissive. In fact, some kids actually pester the bully. This creates a form of 'dance macabre' where the behaviour of each reinforces the other. Other targets appear magnetised to the bully instead of just moving on: 'She is my friend even though she bullies me sometimes'.

Some children stay in the bully–target situation even when there are opportunities for them to get away, maybe because they need to release their anger, be provocative and prolong the encounter. They can also swap roles.

Encourage your child to move away from the bullying game or give her strict instructions not to speak to the bully. She can then communicate nonverbally – but it won't last long.

Parents and kids activity

Rule 3: Let's pretend it's not happening

Most children need to belong to a group, so negative attention is better than none. In this game, the target feels obliged out of fear or favour to defend and protect the bully. Some targets prefer being bullied by popular kids than affiliating with the 'nerds'. They prolong their agony and allow the bully to continue her destructive behaviours. Thus it is easy for the bully to deny, with a look, gesture or words, that she was doing anything. This makes it difficult for teachers to identify the bully. The child denies what is happening or, once confronted, claims that it doesn't affect her. She pretends it was a joke or that everyone was just fooling around.

Parents and kids activity

Adults need to identify and challenge these irrational thoughts. Perhaps you can demonstrate to the child that the 'nerds' are more likely to be successful in 15 years' time, not the bullies.

Rule 4: Let's make it easy for the bully

Bullies are lazy and don't want to think. They want to press a few buttons, have a quick game and obtain instant gratification. The average school bully isn't very creative or intelligent, and lacks verbal skills. She may tease a child about being fat, stupid or gay; the words belong to an average of just four to six different categories. Something the target does makes it easy for the bully to instantly identify her sensitivities. Then the bully uses whatever works to obtain the desired reaction. She wants the target to feel bad, and others to recognise her power. Once thwarted, bullies give up and look for someone else who is vulnerable.

Parents and kids activity

Use the tease list in Chapter 12 to identify your child's sensitivities. Then discuss, de-sensitise her and provide her with options to respond.

Rule 5: Bullies prefer isolated targets

Bullies like picking on children who don't belong to a close, social group. Deep down, they are terrified of being excluded by the tribe, so children who don't belong to a group symbolise their own fears. Many targets are socially quieter, have social difficulties, are more isolated and lack a support network. Their peers can't protect them because they don't have a close connection with them, they don't know how to help, or they fear retaliation. A lone best friend is insufficient to stop the average bully. When the target has a bunch of good friends, the bully has to confront her support group and tends to give up.

Encourage the target to make a bunch of supportive friends (see Chapter 13) and ask her teacher to create a buddy support group.

Parents and kids activity

Rule 6: Witnesses have power

Like the cheering crowd at the theatre or the football, most bullying is conducted in front of peers, onlookers or bystanders. Some bullies are popular and have strong leadership skills. They are supported by their friends and can manipulate a crowd. If the peer group cackles, condones, colludes or collaborates, the bullying escalates. The group allows the bully to manipulate them to build her social power. Bystanders, peers and witnesses can support the bully and deny the bullying to a teacher. But if the peer group challenges the bully and condemns that behaviour, the bullying diminishes. The bully has to change her behaviour to maintain membership of the group. Schools, in turn, need to train bystanders to intervene fairly and responsibly. Students should request and expect assistance from their friends, or move on and make better friends.

Non-bullying interaction

- Family and friends banter all the time and label it 'fooling around' or 'chit-chat'. Children regard banter as being friendly, having fun and a group activity, just like rough play between lion cubs. Although bantering can hurt, children need to identify the difference between social bantering, rough play and nasty bullying.

- One incident of violence is not necessarily bullying.

- Children need to be flexible and socialise with a variety of playmates or friends and respect their rights to socialise with others. Although friendship groups change constantly, children should not be ejected or rejected.

- Children shouldn't be handcuffed to one friend; they shouldn't resent a friend who plays with other friends.

- Children should not ignore another child who has invited them to play, as that child may feel hurt and retaliate by bullying.

- When a friendship ends following an argument, children should move on instead of retaliating or prolonging the connection by bullying.

Key points

- Bullying is an abuse of power.
- It ranges from social banter, teasing, exclusion and harassment to physical violence and crime.
- Some bully for fun but don't mean to hurt, others enjoy causing pain and do it for personal gain.
- Bullying can occur at school, in transit and in the local community.
- Boys and girls may bully differently due to the different structure of their peer groups.

What to do

- Identify the signs of bullying.
- Help your child describe his or her bullying experiences.
- Help your child avoid the bullying games.

2

Bullies and targets

Warren has an odd relationship with Tom. They used to be close friends but their relationship changed once Tom joined the cool group. Warren hangs around Tom and his mates when they play sport. Warren hates it when Tom pushes him away or when the boys physically knock him around. Tom and his crew don't like Warren – they call him a 'geek'. Despite these negative vibes, Warren believes their attention is better than nothing. Unconsciously, he prefers to be alienated by a popular group than to be associated with a bunch of 'nerds'. Tom and his mates actually bully him more than they want to. They explained to the counsellor that he really annoys them, and they are heartily sick of him. Warren told the counsellor he is just trying to be friendly, and they are nasty to him.

About the bully

How to spot a bully

- aims to dominate, command and control others

- has minimal empathy

- bullies siblings and parents

- has an inflated self-opinion

- his schoolwork and school behaviour deteriorates

- associates with mean friends he doesn't invite home

- denies responsibility for his behaviour and blames others

- may boast about his bullying exploits

- 'sucks up' to teachers and parents – is superficially nice

- shows limited remorse

- is secretive about after-school activities

- has unaccounted extra money or gifts, e.g. from extortion or stealing

- offers devious and dishonest answers, and

- resists compliance and cooperation with parents and teachers.

Bullying behaviour

- bully's eyes: cold and aggressive, not kind and friendly

- facial muscles: fixed and tense, not relaxed

- mouth: snarls or mean, not pleasant

- body language: dominating and threatening, not calm

- voice and words: demeaning, hurtful, aggressive, not friendly

- manipulates target and cronies into a state of regular fear

- blackmails target with words or gestures, e.g. 'Say nothing or else!'

- plans his attack

- uses aggression to release negative feelings and resolve conflict

- enjoys abusing his power to dominate, manipulate and hurt, and

- reacts angrily if caught, not sad about hurting someone.

There are many reasons why children bully. A small number are born more aggressive and lacking in empathy. Most are conditioned by their family, school and the prevailing peer norms of behaviour. See Chapters 3 and 9 for further discussion of this.

Types of bullies

Jules is an overweight, awkward boy who has difficulties with schoolwork. His migrant parents work very hard, have little time to help him and don't understand his homework. His grandmother lives with them and idolises his younger sister. She's got the lot: she is pretty, intelligent and has a friendly personality. Jules is frustrated and jealous. His only relief is bullying others less powerful at school. Their pain helps him forget his own.

Bullies come in all shapes and sizes. Most of them are the children we love and care for. But they sometimes misbehave at school like they do at home. It is important for a target to differentiate between kids who enjoy bullying, mean kids who don't care, and careless children who don't realise their behaviours are harmful. Once confronted, the latter are often surprised and ashamed. Thus the target needs to understand that not all bullies are the same. He also needs to understand his role in allowing this game to continue.

There are two main types of bullies:

1. the malicious, or 'saltwater crocodile', and

2. the non-malicious, or 'the fowl that plays foul'.

1. THE SALTWATER CROCODILE

The saltwater crocodile is extremely dangerous and cannot be trusted. If you get caught, then try to escape or fight back, you become history. This malicious bully at school is a sociopath or a psychopath in training. However, if you pretend to be lifeless, the crocodile has been known to lose interest and release people who play dead. Fortunately, only a very small percentage of bullies belong to this group.

Crocodiles:

- have differently wired brains to normal people, affecting their social, emotional and cognitive functions

- are made, not born, and their cunning, aggressive tendencies can begin as early as two years of age

- are more difficult to change the older they become

- lack a conscience and empathy, and enjoy others' pain

- have minimal insight into how others perceive them, e.g. a Queen Bee

- manipulate others with superficial charm

- don't know how to relate effectively, and have poor intimacy skills

- displace their feelings of powerlessness onto someone more vulnerable

- enjoy the challenge of bullying children who fight when attacked or retaliate, and

- may be cruel to animals (usually boys rather than girls).

2. FOWLS THAT PLAY FOUL

There are many types of fowl – here are three examples:

- The peacock that struts his ego around the playground.

- The chicken that gradually pecks away at the weaker ones until it destroys them.

- The lyrebird that copies others and goes with the flow.

These bullies are basically non-malicious: they say things like, 'We were just having a bit of fun', 'We didn't mean to hurt', or 'If you can't take it, leave the group'. They are your ordinary, everyday bullies, your children, cousins and neighbours as well as their current or former best friends. They:

- believe their actions are non-toxic

- assume the target is a willing participant in the game

- claim that they have no intention of hurting the target

- appear oblivious to their target's vulnerabilities

- may or may not have empathy for others' feelings

- tease to connect, flirt and make friends

- want to be cool, powerful or popular

- tease, exclude, harass or bully when supported by their group

- are bored, looking for action or entertainment (like reality television)

- have a strong need to compete, win or dominate others

- react to a perceived insult, dispute or broken friendship

- view bullying as a way to climb the status ladder (especially true of ex-targets). They say, 'If you can't beat them, join them'

- sense at an unconscious level that they are taking power away from the target

- may or may not have emotional problems

- switch 'on and off' – sometimes friendly, sometimes not, and

- are ashamed once their behaviours are exposed.

About the target

How to spot a target

A bully needs the following behaviours from a target. Ask your child's friends, classmates and teachers about whether she exhibits them.

- eyes red, teary, narrowed or wide open, looking down or away

- face white or red, with tense muscles

- lips tight or mouth open

- head down, looking away

- shoulders slumped, bent over or pulled back

- body movements paralysed, rigid or fidgeting, walking off

- voice very quiet, angry, upset, muffled, grunting

- retaliates verbally by blabbing, blaming or criticising back

- feelings are exposed: fear, anger, hurt, hate, embarrassment, teariness, frustration, and

- does nothing, looks like a rabbit in the headlights, walks away or retaliates.

How you become a target

You:

- identify a mean kid but don't think that she will hurt you

- disregard the bully's feedback that she wants to annoy or upset you

- feel sorry for a kid with problems who bullies back

- try to please others to be accepted, but become vulnerable

- try to join a group that doesn't want you

- don't know what to do and remain powerless

- can't avoid danger and protect yourself

- become outraged that you were bullied, especially when you did nothing

- prefer to fight back, get hurt, than enjoy a normal life with real friends

- ignore your survival instinct and fight back when inappropriate, and

- behave like a victim, not a warrior.

Warning signs

Any one of the following symptoms may indicate bullying. Discuss them with your child.

PHYSICAL SIGNS

- Possessions are missing, damaged, scattered, e.g. books, money, clothes, lunch.

- Has bruises, cuts, scratches, torn clothing without a natural explanation.

- Describes being pushed, shoved, punched, hit and kicked.

- Is involved in fights in which she feels powerless.

- Complains of minor aches and pains, often sick with minor health difficulties.

- Sleeps poorly, begins (or resumes) bedwetting and has bad dreams.

- Appears pale, tense or frustrated.

- Makes unusual requests for money.

- Is ravenous after school (if her lunch or lunch money is stolen) or has no appetite.

- Is suddenly late for school, takes an unusual route or prefers to be driven.

- Tries to stay close to a teacher or other adults during breaks.

- Has poor communication skills: limited eye contact, bad posture, jiggles around, mumbles.

ACADEMIC SIGNS

- Has sudden difficulty asking or answering questions in class.

- Does not participate in class activities or interact with peers in class.

- Exhibits a sudden deterioration in class work and/or homework.

- Lacks motivation.
- Is not achieving her potential.

EMOTIONAL SIGNS

- Appears anxious, distressed, uptight.
- Appears sad, depressed, teary, withdrawn, secretive.
- Has sudden changes in behaviour, e.g. is moody, or 'bottles it up and bursts'.
- Is more irritable or angry than usual, sarcastic, over-reacting.
- Denies and says, 'I'm okay', despite symptoms of anger or sadness.
- Is upset after a phone call, text message or email.
- Is unhappier at the end of weekends or holidays before returning to school.
- Is very unhappy at school – 'I don't like that school, I want to leave'.
- Starts to talk about herself in derogatory ways, e.g. 'I'm stupid', 'No-one likes me', 'I don't have any friends'.

SOCIAL SIGNS

- Is made fun of and laughed at in a sarcastic, unfriendly manner.
- Is teased, taunted, ridiculed, degraded, threatened.
- Feels embarrassed, ridiculed or humiliated at school.
- Is socially isolated, has limited contact with classmates at recess, lunchtime and after school hours.
- Is chosen last for a team, project, game, or for sharing a cabin at camp.
- Stops talking about other students and social events.
- Receives mystery phone calls with hang-ups.
- Becomes difficult at home or bullies siblings.

Shy child checklist

Shy kids are more likely to be bullied. Ask your child if any of the following statements applies to her:

- You don't feel motivated to try your best with schoolwork or homework.

- You are scared to participate in class or ask for help.

- You don't know how to start a conversation and chat.

- Lunch and recess is spent alone: in the library, computer room, walking the yard.

- You can't join a group and have fun.

- You don't know how to make a bunch of real friends.

- It's hard to make social arrangements, e.g. phone or text someone.

- You don't like being excluded, alone or bored.

- You put up with one clingy or bossy friend.

- It's easier to mix with younger children or adults than with kids your own age.

- Your self-esteem is poor.

- You've had enough of being pushed around, teased or bullied.

- Being shy is painful.

- You are sad, scared and lonely.

Some children are born shy or socially anxious, others become shy due to a series of events. All shy children are affected by the social behaviours they experience around them. Some very shy people can speak in front of thousands of people but not in front of their own family. Shy children don't necessarily lack confidence; they lack skills. You can use the 'Six Secrets of Relating' in Part Three of this book to help your child improve her social skills.

Key points

■ There are two main types of bullies.

■ Bullies and targets often exhibit telltale signs.

■ Sensitive kids make easy targets.

What to do

• Use the profiles in this chapter to assess whether your child is bullying, being bullied or both – and see elsewhere in the book for the appropriate action to take.

• Teach your child how to identify a mean or a merely inconsiderate bully.

3

What causes bullying?

John was born in Singapore to a Japanese mother and an American father. He went to preschool in Singapore and then to a Canadian school for a few years. Each time his family relocated to another culture, he felt increasingly different to other children. It was stressful to balance his family's internal cultural conflicts and simultaneously deal with the cultural differences in each school. Then his father was transferred to Australia. Once he entered this new 'rough 'n ready' environment, his low self-esteem attracted the school bullies. His cultural upbringing prevented him from speaking out and obtaining help until he broke down.

There are many different causes of bullying. History and psychology have proved the power of the group to alienate and abuse those who are vulnerable or different. Bullying occurs within a context of intertwining systems. Basically these include the state system, which reflects local laws and culture, the school system and the family system. The result is that people learn how to remain aggressive or become powerless and passive. Later on (see Chapter 9) I will provide some explanations to help your child understand why he is bullied or why he bullies.

There will always be bullying. However, once you understand the causes, you can work out how to prevent it and how to intervene appropriately.

The bullying paradox

Children are competitive. They copy adult role models to be the best and get the best. They exclude and devalue to maintain their power in the tribe. Bullying has long been regarded as part of growing up. In fact, 'bully for you' is a form of support for an act of bravado. Bullying is evident in the animal kingdom, in parliament and in sport, and is known as 'survival of the fittest'. It reflects the adversarial masculine approach of the hunter and the hunted, not the collaborative, feminine approach of the gatherer.

The paradoxical attitude of prizing and protecting bullies while simultaneously condemning them fosters a conspiracy of silence. Bullying becomes secret, invisible and condoned by society.

It appears that most humans are social animals who survive in their tribe when they subscribe to group norms. If they are in a tolerant tribe, they behave with respect and empathy. But if they are forced to survive in a hostile environment, they collude with the leaders, sacrifice their moral values and sabotage their peers. Most kids are affected by *where* they are, not who they are.

Cultural factors

From the hill tribes of Vietnam to the inner city of Leicester to the suburbs of Melbourne, schools mirror their social and cultural environment, which, in turn, influence the school community. And the social environment is less than ideal: despite human rights legislation, children are still treated as second-class citizens, and women still have less power than men. Although parts of the media and policies such as multiculturalism foster diversity, adults still bully those who are different.

The role of the school

The 'Three Monkeys' symbolise 'See no evil, hear no evil, speak no evil'. Pat Ferris has applied this concept to workplace bullying; it also provides a handy description of how schools approach it.

See no evil – do nothing

Bullying is a tradition in many schools. It tends to be worse in schools that either admire, condone, tolerate, deny or do nothing about bullying. These schools do not value mutual respect and have low levels of pro-social behaviour. They allow discrimination and favouritism. There is also a cultural element: males should be tough, it's 'weak' or 'sissy' to complain. Students who can't stand up for themselves are regarded as 'girly' and 'gutless'.

Bullies generally operate out of the teacher's sight, and will 'suck up' to teachers to fool them. Teachers become oblivious to the reality. Bullies know they can get away with it because the school won't intervene. Reporting stops when witnesses aren't protected and nothing is done.

Bullying can metastasise in any direction. In many schools, students, teachers and parents use bullying tactics in the classroom, staffroom, carpark, office or at parent social events. They can actively or passively encourage students, staff or parents to attack a target.

Hear no evil – a superficial attempt

These schools may have a written policy, and occasionally invite an expert speaker to entertain the students (who regard it as a bludge period and quickly forget it). They may force the poor target and the bully to 'talk it out' in a teacher's office, focus on one method to solve all difficulties, or discipline the bully with a word of warning. Their staff, student and parent training is limited. They may develop programmes for students while bullying staff and neglecting parents. They lack consistency across the whole school, perhaps dealing with one year level while neglecting the others. They can follow fads or fashions without proper investigation.

Many schools dislike the word 'bullying', because they fear negative publicity and object to its wider humanitarian implication. They camouflage their policies and programmes, e.g. 'building resilience and pro-social skills'. The toxic message about bullying can be lost in translation.

Speak no evil – consistent, effective measures to reduce bullying

These schools realise that bullying happens and requires constant vigilance and collaboration between staff, students, parents and the community e.g. police, law and media. The school relies upon its philosophies, policies and programmes to create a culture and climate where everyone is valued and treated with respect. They reflect safety, equality and diversity. They demonstrate to all children and their families that bullying is unacceptable. They constantly review, monitor and maintain their anti-bullying programmes.

Other school factors

THE PRINCIPAL

The principal or headteacher is like the conductor of an orchestra. He (or she) translates the state and school board requirements and expectations into school-friendly practices. He needs to coordinate all sections of the school, from staff and students to secretaries, and he needs to be vigilant in monitoring the quality of respect and justice for the whole school. When the school has a responsible principal who provides a strong leadership model, there is less bullying. When he is aggressive or passive, bullying is enabled.

PARENTS

The research clearly shows that schools should develop a closer working relationship with parents to reduce bullying. However, schools don't systematically involve them. So one of the major circumstantial causes of bullying is not involved in the solution!

THE PEER GROUP

The cool, sporty, tough, popular group occupies the idolised position, the middle group represents the majority of students, and the less popular groups ('nerds', 'losers') gather in the rejected zone. Students use the group to establish their social status. They connect, devalue and exclude to raise their profile. The groups, gangs or cliques change constantly. Bullies use the group to maintain their power and social status. If the peer group giggles out of fear, embarrassment or amusement, it rewards the bully. Some reinforce the bully's power by joining in. When bystanders do nothing, the bullying escalates. When bystanders intervene and challenge, it stops.

Review your child's school

- Does the school implement anti-bullying policies for everyone?

- Is the school vigilant and consistent in its actions?

- Does the principal actively discourage bullying?

- Does the school follow through on complaints?

- Do children feel safe or do they leave because of bullying?

The role of the family

Children are a reflection of their family. They inherit genes, predispositions, attitudes and behaviours that affect their likelihood of remaining resilient in the face of bullying or increase their likelihood of becoming a target, a bully or both. Let's look at this major influence on their behaviour.

The deluxe model

The democratic family functions best with the stresses of today's society. Children receive encouragement, praise, rewards and consequences. In this family, activities and duties, skills and difficulties are discussed openly and regularly. Children are heard and respected. They learn how to discuss problems and how to obtain help in solving them. Parents who use democratic discipline don't need to bully. These family systems have firm, fair, clearly established boundaries and guidelines. If children break the rules and hurt others, they face consequences.

They also learn from their families how to accept, respect and protect themselves. They are less likely to be bullied because they are accustomed to having their say, standing up for themselves and dealing with difficult people. Likewise, they are less overprotected and less likely to bully because they are brought up with firm, consistent behaviour boundaries. When they treat others without empathy, there are consequences for inappropriate behaviours.

Siblings

A child is affected by her position within the family and the ages of her siblings. A significant age gap between the siblings positions the younger one to become a 'pseudo-adult', overprotected but socially neglected. She confronts less competition and fewer responsibilities, and has less opportunity to develop assertive social skills. Single children may lack the social survival techniques that come from daily skirmishes with siblings.

Parents' ages

Many parents are having children later nowadays, due to re-marriage and career reasons. Although older parents may have more time, they often treat their children as equals: they have less energy to establish firm behaviour boundaries, and they become lax, overprotective or overcontrolling. Generally, older parents mix with their friends unless they can socialise with others who have children of similar ages, so their children have less opportunity to mix with their peers, but relate well to adults.

The family jigsaw

Parenting is disrupted when there is only one main parent. Separation, divorce, re-partnering and stepsiblings also disrupt traditional parenting and discipline patterns. The child may feel vulnerable, confused, angry, guilty and abandoned. Her self-esteem is lowered and she has less energy to deal with school problems. The child who spends time with both parents has to adjust to different parenting styles, including the handling of love and discipline. Some children rely upon one parent but, unlike other kids, they can't afford to stress their main caregiver. They have fewer boundaries but less opportunity to challenge their sole parent, and thus to develop assertiveness skills.

Grandparents

Some children are raised mainly by grandparents. Unfortunately, grandparents can confuse the child and sabotage the parents' role. They can spoil, overprotect and indulge, but provide fewer boundaries and less discipline. Inadvertently, this lowers a child's self-esteem and her ability to handle difficult people. If grandparents are traditional, overcontrolling and less flexible, they won't provide opportunities for the child to challenge them, which is essential for an assertive, confident child.

Parental difficulties

When parents have difficulties, their children are affected. The social child goes out with friends and switches off; the sensitive, shy, enmeshed child stays at home and worries. Parents with difficulties use this child to balance the tension between them, and the child become emotionally entrapped or involved with adult problems that she is ill-equipped to handle. Her self-esteem suffers and she has less energy to deal with school problems like bullying. If one parent, generally the mother, is bullied by the other, usually the male partner, children learn aggression and powerlessness.

Family changes

Unfortunately, many children don't develop social survival skills naturally. I cite three reasons to explain this.

1. THE BREAK-UP OF THE EXTENDED FAMILY

Since World War Two the extended family has experienced huge changes. Close extended families provide children with opportunities to express their real feelings and relate at a more intimate level. Regular family get-togethers oblige them to relate to different types of people, nice and nasty, simple and complicated. At any family function, children banter and tease, argue and fight, then make up and laugh together – all within a brief period. Whereas, in families who encounter their extended family only at weddings, funerals, or for a toxic few hours at Christmas, Thanksgiving or Easter, their opportunities to relate are severely handicapped.

2. CHANGES IN THE NUCLEAR FAMILY

Over the past few decades this close, core unit has changed and now functions differently, including the obvious change of divorce and re-marriage. Many children have no father, while their single mother is stressed, depressed or traumatised. Modern technology has reduced the need for regular family activities like washing the dishes together. Most parents are very busy, and many are bogged down by their responsibilities. They rely on their partner, relatives or childcare, and are unavailable for hands-on involvement with their children. They create fewer opportunities to develop consistent discipline systems. Their children lack the opportunity to learn how to respect others and to then internalise their personal and social boundaries. Alternatively, parents belong to the 'me' generation and often spend more time developing their own needs, which leaves less time for parenting their children. They overcompensate by spoiling their children, turning them into 'PIT' ('prince/princess-in-training') bullies.

At dinnertime, instead of chatting around the kitchen table, children are confronted with a kitchen bench, a television or meal shifts. There is less family time for talking and mutual support.

Stressed children are forced to share their school problems during the time available between their parents' flexi-working hours, chauffeuring to numerous after-school activities, the car radio or between mobile phone calls. Unless the shy, insecure target is given the opportunity during a meal or at other special sharing times (like bedtime), she may try once or twice to tell her parents, but then give up.

3. THE ELECTRONIC 'BLAH BLAH' REVOLUTION

Instead of encouraging valuable socialising time, many parents want their children to be 'safe' inside, so they replace the social void with the toys of the electronic revolution: all-day cyber babysitting screens, computer games and television.

Too much electronic time can lead to depression, social isolation and loneliness. The microchip seems to have created a generation of angry boys who have little exercise or emotional release, except to fight back, while girls watch enormous amounts of television instead of playing with siblings or neighbours (see Chapter 6). In fact, the microchip itself has created a new type of abusive power. Cyber bullying is devious, unavoidable, and invades a child's safest retreats. Malicious rumours can be spread quickly to a large audience at any time; anonymous messages can be devastating.

The core issues

It is sometimes hard to understand the formation of targets, bullies and children who use both types of behaviours. Here are some guidelines.

The target

Dan Olveus, the Norwegian anti-bullying pioneer, believes that many targets come from overprotective families. This includes the cautious, sensitive child who has a close relationship with Mum and an emotionally distant father; and families who cocoon their children, e.g. the 'special' child. Others come from caring but quiet, shy homes with little need to practise confronting stressful encounters and restricted opportunities for socialising outside their nuclear family. Some have controlling, traditional or insecure parents who can't tolerate a difference of opinion. Others have parents who experience(d) victimisation and powerlessness, and transmit their fear to their children. Many children believe that their health, financial and other family difficulties make the bullying insignificant, so they don't tell their parents about the bullying. Help is delayed or denied. Finally, if a child can't stand up to the parents he loves and say 'No', then he can't stand up to bullies he hates and say 'Don't'.

The reactive target

This child is a target and a bully at different times. She is unpredictable; many such children are self-involved, show minimal interest in others, and have poor self-esteem and social difficulties. Some react to a personal, family or other difficulty, past or present, by becoming aggressive instead of assertive. They are often disliked by adults. They may have learning difficulties, concentration difficulties or be immature, hyperactive, attention-seeking. They are overly sensitive to banter or criticism; they blame the absence of justice and fight back, thereby prolonging the bullying game.

Their parents may provide opposing or inconsistent role models. They can't express their feelings in a constructive, assertive manner, so their children resort to a cocktail of passive and aggressive behaviours at school and at home. Some angry parents then maintain this role model by sabotaging or suing the school.

The bully

The trend is clear. Although a few children are born with psychopathic tendencies, the majority learn how to be bullies from the role models at home and school. They are trained by unhappy, dysfunctional or broken families. Love, acceptance and respect are disguised or conditional. They can be victimised or bullied themselves. The child learns that bullying is okay because his parents don't expect him to show empathy for others. Nor does he learn how to respect those who are handicapped, different or gifted. He becomes intolerant, racist, chauvinistic, homophobic or discriminatory.

Others have passive parents who deny, who show little interest in their child's misbehaviours, and who won't discipline them. They spoil them in order to compensate for their difficulty in providing on-the-job parenting. These children have no behaviour boundaries or consistent guidelines: one day they can get away with bashing their younger brother, the next day they can't. Some learn from their families how to enjoy watching targets suffer, while some parents value aggression in their child – 'You showed them'.

The end result is obvious. The bully copies his significant role models. No-one has made him accountable for his bullying behaviours or demonstrated more effective ways of releasing negative feelings and relating to people. The cycle then continues when the bully is shamed and blamed.

Some questions for your family

- How does the family enable a child to become a target, a bully or both?

- What influences cannot be changed? (e.g. older parents, siblings)

- What influences can be changed? (e.g. role models, discipline)

- Who is being unfairly blamed?

- What skills does the target or bully need to learn?

Key points

- Aggression has a cultural and a biological foundation.
- Bullying is enabled by state and local cultural systems.
- School action ranges from denial and tokenism to consistency.
- Schools must involve all parents and students to combat bullying.
- The family has had many structural changes in the past decades.
- Family role models can facilitate vulnerability and abuse.

What to do

- Consider how your family can assist your child.
- Consider how the school can involve students, staff, family and community.
- Investigate local and state-wide anti-bullying guidelines. Are they constructive – e.g. do they respect natural and restorative justice, and have adequate funding? Or are they destructive – e.g. is there zero tolerance (which enables bullies and takes targets' power away), limited funding, and tokenism?
- Check out other useful community structures – e.g. the school board directors' responsibilities, school–police services, the media.

4

The damage done

John was bullied at school every day for eight years. They called him a 'stupid, fat wog'. He was excluded and physically pushed around. He felt like the class buffoon or punching bag. The teachers often joined in, and even instigated some attacks. Following his suicide attempt, John finally left that school.

Now that he is suing the school for disregarding his welfare, he is aware of how his obsessive behaviours, poor social life and fear of others mocking him resulted from the bullying. Despite being a successful lawyer, every day he recalls his horrible experiences.

Nobody enjoys being bullied. When a child believes that she has been bullied and feels hurt, vulnerable and powerless, many different groups of people can be affected. These include the target, the bully, the reactive target, parents, siblings, teachers, peer group, onlookers, school and community.

The many painful experiences include:

- the child's perception of the actual bullying experience

- a single, painful event can be traumatic but discounted ('It only happened once')

- powerlessness: any attempt she makes to block the bullying fails

- the effort it takes to pretend it isn't happening or to deny it

- difficulty reporting at school and at home because it's too painful ('I don't want to talk about it')

- the inability to express the sheer depth of her pain to anyone

- hating feeling ashamed, humiliated and a failure

- fear and embarrassment about requesting help ('Please don't tell my parents or the school…')

- fear of future attacks (which exacerbates their impact)

- when she risks seeking help and fails, she feels betrayed and abandoned ('Nobody can help me, I am alone to be attacked again…')

- peers witness her emotional and social vulnerability; some join the attack, while others distance themselves

- as the bullying continues, the damage escalates, other activities deteriorate and the situation worsens – her level of fear, frustration and powerlessness increases

- many may still minimise their painful experiences/feelings – 'I'm okay, I can cope. I still want to stay at this school because I have friends' (who don't support them)

- targets become paralysed or else retaliate

- when superficial anti-bullying policies, programmes and crisis intervention procedures fail, the target feels bullied by the school – 'It wasn't fair', and

- those who fight back or provoke may feel guilty and become hostile to professional assistance – 'Why do I have to be here talking about it? It's too painful'.

Consequences for the target

All types of bullying can injure a child. The impact will be affected by the target's personality, the support provided by the school and the parents, the peer group reaction and the bully's style. (The most painful form of bullying is teasing: its impact can linger the longest.)

Immediate consequences

When Jodie was bullied, she went a deep shade of pink, her eyes watered, her voice trembled and her mouth twitched. She looked scared, sensitive and vulnerable.

Targets don't look, sound or behave like normal, happy children. You can see they have difficulty coping. Their eyes, face, skin tone, body language, voice and words *broadcast* their fear, anger, distress and powerlessness. When a child is injured, it will be evident in some or all of the following areas.

PHYSICAL

Judith was five years old and quite babyish. Some other children forced her to eat dirt, pinched and punched her. As a result, she was wetting her bed and complained of stomach pains.

Targets of physical bullying may suffer the following consequences:

- cuts, scratches, bruises or other wounds
- headaches, backaches, stomach aches
- bedwetting, soiling
- loss of hair, skin disorders
- sleep difficulties, nightmares
- menstruation difficulties
- loss of appetite or over-eating to compensate
- pale, taut and tense appearance
- poor posture, stooped, and
- stress hormones reduce the immune system's ability to combat viruses and other infections, so children are more likely to become ill.

INTELLECTUAL

Jenny was a bright girl who could have gone to university but she never achieved her potential because of the teasing and exclusion. She finished school with mediocre grades.

The immediate intellectual consequences include:

- Suffers reduced concentration, learning and memory difficulties.

- Lacks motivation to work or enjoy his studies.

- Focuses solely on his studies but avoids extra-curricular activities.

- Attends class irregularly and misses out on schoolwork.

- Moves to a new school to avoid bullying but takes time to settle in and adjust to a new curriculum.

- Unless very diligent or intelligent, his emotions handicap his studies.

- Most children want to be like everybody else. They might do their work but keep a low profile. Targets don't question, contribute or complain to avoid attracting attention. Their schoolwork suffers.

- The child with learning difficulties hides his disabilities for fear of being called 'stupid', so is denied extra assistance.

- Gifted, intelligent, sensitive children fear exposing their knowledge. They dread being ridiculed by jealous students. They don't develop their potential; they disguise their unique talents and restrict their achievements. Everyone misses out.

- Although cooperative learning in a group is an excellent way to learn, some children fear group work where they are expected to do all the difficult work, and thus risk criticism or mockery.

- Sensitive children fear all feedback, even if it's constructive. They sabotage their learning by hiding their thoughts in order to reduce further feedback.

- Teachers assume that the bright, bored, quiet or shy target is content. They under- or overestimate the target's abilities, instead of providing extra help or extension studies.

SOCIAL

Jason was teased about his family name. He avoided the playground at lunchtime and escaped into a computer. He was lonely but left alone. Following five counselling sessions, he blocked the bullies. Now he spends lunchtime with four quiet friends. They talk about computers, go to weekend computer markets together, and work on their software collection at home. He is enjoying his social life.

- Bullying handicaps social skills, and children with poor social skills are more likely to be bullied.

- The average child feels uncomfortable around tense, uptight children and rejects them; perhaps he doesn't trust or respect them. (Maybe they remind him of his own vulnerabilities.)

- Some targets remain padlocked to one friend, whom they obey in order to prolong the friendship. They are too scared to express their opinions, possibly lose this friend and be alone.

- Some kids trail after a trendy group, believing it's better to be bullied by the popular kids than to be associated with nice 'nerds'.

- When targets inadvertently set themselves up to be bullied repeatedly, they get sucked into a destructive downward spiral. As the bullying escalates, the target becomes more vulnerable and powerless, thus his peer group rejects him.

- Many targets socialise with children who have poor social skills and who congregate at the bottom of the social ladder. Unlike most normal friendships, where children support and protect one another, these students can't support the target.

- They are the last to be chosen to join a group project, join a game, or share a cabin at camp.

- Their social life on the weekend or holidays is poor. They are not invited to parties or sleepovers.

- Targets may feel safe at home or with special friends, but fear bullying elsewhere.

- Some targets are scared of being hurt again and stop socialising, becoming shy dropouts or socially isolated.

- Targets may have difficulty establishing normal friendships because they forget how to socialise.

- Some targets are so traumatised that they can't establish friendships once the bullying stops.

SELF-ESTEEM

Bella used to be friendly and gregarious. Although she is now at a lovely, friendly school, the painful bullying she experienced at her last school has left her quiet, shy, unfriendly and alone. She feels bad that although she has moved schools, she still can't cope or make friends.

- Many children are teased because something about them is different. If they don't accept this difference, their sensitivity invites further teasing, especially when peers harass and exaggerate it. This lowers their self-esteem.

- While their internal bully constantly harasses and reminds them of their personal inadequacies, the school bully identifies their sensitive points and targets them mercilessly.

- Children with poor self-esteem display a sign saying, 'I don't like myself'. Other children think, 'If you don't like yourself, why should I like you? So I'll treat you as you treat yourself.'

- Targets blame themselves for not blocking the bullying like other children seem to. This reinforces their feeling of being different, and their self-esteem falls further.

- They become extremely sensitive to criticism and reject even constructive feedback that would improve their social survival skills.

- Their self-esteem deteriorates as they become embarrassed, lose confidence and give up. They find it hard to be open and sharing or trust others.

- They become self-centred, extremely sensitive or critical of everything they do.

- They despise their personality, rejecting themselves as well as others. They become lonely.

EMOTIONAL/PSYCHOLOGICAL

Tom is a nervous target. He can't sit still and he constantly interrupts other kids by saying stupid things in class. He is terrified of being bullied again.

- The target moves into survival mode when bullied or threatened. His body is regulated by its 'fight or flight' instinct to protect itself. Thus, other bodily functions close down: he can't breathe deeply, his shallow breathing reduces his oxygen intake, so he has insufficient breath to neutralise stress hormones.

- His painfully high level of fear and anxiety sabotages a state of calm. He can't be relaxed or easy-going, which is essential for socialising.

- He can become very frustrated or angry at being manipulated by the bully and others (e.g. their school).

- Some react and retaliate, exacerbating the situation by becoming aggressive or provocative.

- Others bottle their tension up at school, then release it at home by being rude, hostile and angry.

- He feels confused, stuck, powerless and doesn't know what to do, so he does nothing.

- He cannot express or release his pain and discomfort. He speaks very quietly, quickly and muffles his words. No-one can validate his feelings.

- His emotional burnout leads to denial and disassociation.

- Some internalise their anger and become sad, miserable, mildly depressed and teary.

Symptoms of longer-term psychological damage

The body responds to extreme stress by 'releasing a cascade of cortisol, adrenaline and other hormones that can damage brain cells, impair memory and set in motion a long-lasting and worsening disregulation of the body's complex biochemistry'. Many targets pollute their bodies with surplus stress hormones when they deny their anger, fear and sadness. This is reflected in their behaviours. They develop defence mechanisms and psychological symptoms to cope, such as panic attacks, butterflies in their stomach, perspiration, blushing, obsessive thoughts and behaviours. These symptoms can lead to severe anxiety disorders and other psychological or pathological damage. The following problems are often seen in bullying targets:

- *School refusal and school phobia.* Many children who have been bullied stay away from school occasionally or regularly, using excuses like, 'I'm not feeling well', 'I haven't done my homework', 'We aren't doing much work today' and 'I don't want to go to that school'.

- *Shyness and social phobia.* Targets who are terrified of again being bullied restrict or avoid social interactions with peers. They carry their shyness or social anxiety into adulthood, and some develop a fear of relating to strangers.

- *Post-traumatic stress disorder.* Some targets experience a life-threatening situation, where they feel exposed to an actual or possible threat, abuse or serious injury. They may re-experience unpleasant memories of the event in bad dreams and flashbacks. They avoid situations that bring back memories of the bullying. They may become hypersensitive, hypervigilant, emotional, angry and disconnected from others. Their concentration and memory can be affected. Targets require therapy to deal with this level of trauma.

- *Learned helplessness.* In situations of prolonged abuse and trauma, the brain releases less cortisol, which causes permanent neurological damage and perhaps a state of 'learned helplessness'. Some children will feel as though they have been tied up in a straitjacket or betrayed by adults who won't protect them. They become even more helpless every time the bullying occurs again (even at a new school) because they lack bully-blocking skills. Generally, children blame themselves, not their parents, teachers, peers or school.

- *Depression, suicidal tendencies, suicide and murder.* The bullied child can internalise his anger and sadness. He develops a mild or serious depression, and appears slow, tired, snappy or agitated. Bullying can lead to thoughts and acts of self-destruction, self-mutilation and suicide. There are also horrific examples of targets who retaliate by killing teachers and peers and then taking their own lives.

The damage can linger into adulthood

Bullying can harm targets for years after leaving school. It can lead to low self-esteem and social isolation in adulthood.

- *Relationships.* Shy, bullied survivors may find it difficult to establish healthy relationships. Men may lose the confidence to establish a sexual identity; some never marry or partner. Others attract partners who manipulate and bully them. Consequently, their self-esteem and respect for their partner deteriorates. The relationship suffers.

- *Career.* Targets don't always reach their academic potential due to stress, poor concentration, motivation and depression. Others lack the social skills to manage difficult people. This limits their choice of career.

- *Workplace bullying.* More people get bullied at work than at school. Workplace bullying is extremely traumatic for targets: they have more to lose and the damage is often greater, as the injuries can be worse than with school bullying. Resolution and treatment may take many years.

How bullying affects others

Bullying is like a bomb which splinters in all directions. It damages targets and their families, their teachers, the school, onlookers, the bully and the community.

- *Families.* Parents, siblings and grandparents can become very upset when a child is affected by school bullying. Besides, children may be teased about a sibling or parent, which will affect their relationship with that person.

- *Teachers and the school.* Bullying destroys respect, wastes money, and reflects bullying in other parts of the school system, e.g. teacher and parent bullying. Some teachers blame themselves for failing to protect the child. And no-one likes the legal repercussions when families sue or the media chases a story.

- *Bystanders/peer group/onlookers.* Most bystanders don't enjoy bullying as a spectator sport or as reality television. They may personally identify with the target. They may fear that if they report the bullying to the school, the bully will target them next or the school won't support them. Alternatively, they fear appearing weak to 'macho' friends and risk losing their status within the group. They can feel scared, powerless, guilty and shameful for doing nothing. When the peer group says that bullying is okay, then it's okay. If they disapprove, then bullying is not okay. Sadly, they don't realise that they create and maintain this social status system.

- *Bullies lose too!* Like their targets, many bullies have difficulties with health, schoolwork, school attendance and low self-esteem. They too can be emotionally neglected, bullied, abused or experience violence and family dysfunction. They have personal, social and interpersonal difficulties. They have difficulties expressing empathy, dealing with their emotions and conflict. Their friends become tired of being manipulated or bullied, and move on. They may experience depression, anxiety, suicidal thoughts and trauma at school and later.

Key points

- Bullying injures children physically, emotionally, academically and socially, and erodes self-esteem.
- Their injuries can become social, psychological and criminal, short- and long-term disorders.
- Bullying affects many different people, e.g. family, teacher, peer group and community.
- Bullies also lose out in a big way.

What to do

- Find out how your child is affected by the bullying.
- Obtain appropriate help for everyone affected.
- Bullies and their families also require help.
- Students need to develop bully-blocking skills wherever they are.

PART TWO

TAKING ACTION

5

First, transform your child's attitudes

As children grow, they gather values and beliefs about how life should be. They absorb attitudes from their family, friends, school, television and society. Clearly the bully has an 'attitude' problem and should develop respect and empathy for others. However, targets also need to change their 'attitude'. They carry faulty thoughts which make it easy for bullies to use them as target practice.

Targets need to 'reprogramme' their negative, powerless attitude before they can change behaviours to block the bullying. They need to accept that bullying happens, consider it carefully and then take effective action. Once they re-adjust their view of themselves and others, they can replace the following faulty attitudes with sensible, self-protective ones. When you change your state of mind, you change your behaviour.

Tell your child: Imagine that a few negative computer programs were implanted into your brain a long time ago. It's time to trash the old stuff that makes a bully happy. Now visualise yourself installing a new program into your brain which takes away the bully's power. This program

Parents and kids activity

empowers you to maintain strong eye contact, look confident, act assertively and give neutral retorts. Once you change the game, you are far less likely to become bully fodder.

'It's bad to be different'

Every child is unique and different. Paradoxically, most children tell their parents they want to be treated as an individual at home, but at school they want to be the same as everyone else. The primitive need to hunt or gather compels children to others who are like them. Anyone who is different may threaten the rest of the tribe. However, what's normal varies from school to school and is created by the peer group.

Parents and kids activity

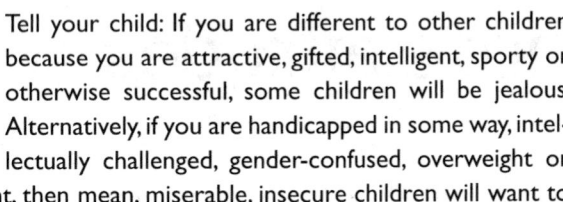

Tell your child: If you are different to other children because you are attractive, gifted, intelligent, sporty or otherwise successful, some children will be jealous. Alternatively, if you are handicapped in some way, intellectually challenged, gender-confused, overweight or culturally different, then mean, miserable, insecure children will want to make you feel bad instead. However, there are always children who are different but who connect with the tribe and don't threaten them.

You need to accept that it is normal to be different, even if you aren't 'average' or 'ordinary'. Although you may be gifted or handicapped in some areas, you are probably very normal in others and share a lot in common with your peers. This includes dealing with the stresses of growing up, homework, chores, hobbies, keeping your room tidy and enjoying your social life.

Be proud that you are unique in some ways and similar to your peers in others. However, you may need to blend in and behave like everyone else, otherwise you could be targeted. You can use your difference – e.g. 'Everyone knows I love to eat' – or disguise your sensitivity about being different – e.g. 'My weird face gives me a lot of attention'. Alternatively, find common areas of interest to show that you are similar to them – e.g. sport, hobbies, ambitions or use social skills to show that you are friendly and caring.

'It's my fault'

Some children are oblivious to the bullying culture. They believe they deserve to be bullied because they are not good enough for the peer group. Some feel ashamed to involve their parents, and guilty when they upset them. This increases the self-blame game and further lowers their self-esteem.

Tell your child: Look for three reasons why you are bullied. If you can't find any in this book, then blame your school, the government or the stars. The important thing is that you don't blame yourself and become stuck and powerless.

Parents and kids activity

Change your attitude about being a target. You will find out that bad things happen to nice people all the time. You have to become resilient and say, 'That's life.'

'I am very sensitive'

Some children are born very sensitive and react to any threatening comment, regardless of its truth or falsehood. Instead of teaching them how to regulate their sensitivities, their parents accommodate them. They say, 'Don't be mean to little Billy because he is very sensitive.' But kids at school don't care. They treat the sensitive child like anyone else.

Tell your child: If bullies say things like, 'You idiot', 'This seat is reserved,' 'You made a mistake...ha ha', 'Go away' or 'You can't play with us today', you may think, 'How dare they treat me like this – my parents wouldn't do this!' It's a real shock. You're not sure

Parents and kids activity

what to do. You react by showing fear, anger, or by doing nothing. The bully senses your vulnerability and attacks.

Apart from your family, close friends and teacher, it is nobody's business what you feel inside. So disguise your sensitivities and trick the bully.

'I don't want to accept the truth'

What a shame we aren't all attractive, intelligent, sporty, trendy or sociable like the popular kids. Most children feel insecure about who they really are or 'should be' while passing through childhood, puberty and adolescence.

Parents and kids activity

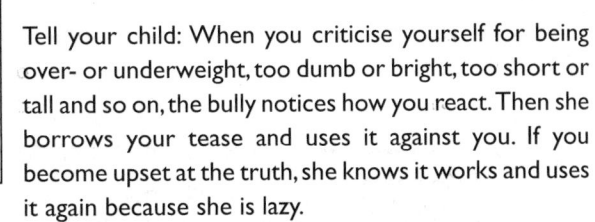

Tell your child: When you criticise yourself for being over- or underweight, too dumb or bright, too short or tall and so on, the bully notices how you react. Then she borrows your tease and uses it against you. If you become upset at the truth, she knows it works and uses it again because she is lazy.

If the comment is true and it hurts, e.g. 'You're fat', then change the truth – diet and exercise. If you can't change it, then accept it and joke about it, e.g. being small, homosexual, different race, religion, coloured. And if it is not true, why bother getting upset?

'How dare they criticise my family!'

Most family members know that they will experience bantering and teasing at one stage or another. Yet children hate hearing members of their family, especially their mother, criticised by others. The same child who calls her mother or sister a 'bitch' or 'tart' at home becomes upset if someone else says, 'Your mother/sister is a slut' or 'Your mother/brother is fat'. The tease is designed to provoke, regardless of truth. The child who dislikes others attacking her family becomes upset, overreacts and fights back. The only thing she proves is her sensitivity. Everyone knows that no family is perfect.

Tell your child: When you accept yourself and your family, you can respond. If you become upset when your family is criticised, discuss family secrets with someone you trust to change your attitude and response.

Parents and kids activity

'I want to do it on my own!'

Some children have been conditioned to behave independently. Sadly, like so many adults, they value the idea of not needing others. However, no-one truly achieves in life without the support of others. Even a bullfighter won't enter the bullring without support staff ready to intervene if there is danger. Nor can a child deal with long-term bullying or harassment on her own. See also Chapter 13.

Tell your child: Use the techniques in this book to begin blocking bullies on your own. At the same time get support, advice or help from others.

Parents and kids activity

'I believe in justice – this isn't fair'

This attitude is also expressed as: 'I'm not hurting them so they shouldn't hurt me', 'I'm just standing up for my rights', 'They always pick on me', 'They started it', 'They should play with me' and 'It's not my fault, I did nothing. The bully should get punished.'

Tell your child: You may have a strong belief in justice, as bullying is an abuse of your human rights. You believe that people shouldn't tease, bully or harass, especially for no reason. You need to accept that bullying happens although the reasons are camouflaged. Everyone bullies

Parents and kids activity

to stay in groups, and the way you behave may show a bully what an easy target you are. Perhaps your social aspirations don't match the group, so it excludes you. Maybe you challenged a bully to prove your rights but instead exacerbated the situation. You know that life isn't fair, so you can't always rely on justice. You need to help yourself and do something constructive to block the bullying.

'I tried something but it didn't work'

Although bullying escalates over a period of time, some children try out a new idea and expect an immediate result.

Parents and kids activity

Tell your child: It's not easy getting the recipe right – for example, maybe you forget to use eye contact, you sound angry or look like limp celery. You could become discouraged with the 'all or nothing' or 'hit or miss' method. You say, 'It didn't work'. No-one can expect instant results, especially without coaching.

When you plan suitable action, take five to ten minutes every day to practise new ideas. Something will improve, but you need to look for small, subtle improvements. It takes time to block bullying effectively.

'Nothing and no-one can help'

Some children believe that their parents, peers and teachers are as helpless as they are. They believe that bullying can't be stopped. Perhaps they were told to do nothing or to fight back, but it didn't work. Maybe the situation was handled poorly and the bullying continued.

Parents and kids activity

Tell your child: Although it may seem pointless to take action when you don't believe anything can be done and it's a waste of time, you don't know what's possible until you try. Just because you feel bad doesn't mean that others are powerless. Even your mother can't always read your mind perfectly, so you can't read someone else's mind. If you believe that no-one can help you, you stop others from trying. You don't know whether they are powerless or not until you try, so don't suffer because you feel powerless. Although you may feel pessimistic, there are some very effective skills in this book which can help you and give others 'a fair go', and allow them to help you.

Write down three faulty beliefs you need to change.

1. ....

2. ....

3. ....

Kids activity

Get rid of bad habits: don't make the bully happy

Parents and kids activity

1. Don't be scared of pain

Children are often scared of life-saving injections, gym exercise to build their muscles, and confronting the dentist. Speaking about bullying is very painful.

Tell your child: You can feel embarrassed, shy or paralysed with fear. Many children say, 'I don't want to talk about it'. They turn their head away or lower their eyes, expecting the subject to close. Unfortunately, if you don't talk about it, the bully knows that you are publicity-shy. The bullying will get worse and you will suffer more.

2. Don't be a belly-button watcher ('BBW' for short)

Some children are very anxious about how they appear to others. They become totally absorbed in their own thoughts and feelings. I call this 'belly-button watching'. They forget to show interest, care and empathy in their classmates.

Tell your child: Be aware that you create real problems when kids try to be friendly with you and you reject their invitations to play. They may retaliate by teasing or excluding you. Besides, if you want to know how to make friends or block bullies, you need to adjust your behaviour according to the feedback you receive from other children. You can't do this if you are belly-button watching.

Don't focus on yourself all the time; show interest and empathy in other children. Use their feedback to guide what you do next.

3. Don't show your fear or anger, or do nothing

I often ask children, 'Why do bullies bully? What do they want kids to do?'

They say things like, 'They want you to get upset, cry or fight back.'

I summarise the essential feelings a bully looks for: 'So a bully wants a kid to get angry, scared or do nothing?' Then I say, 'What do you do – say mean things back, run away, do nothing?'

They tell me what they do. I summarise and boomerang their words back, e.g., 'So you get angry and upset, which makes the bully happy?' Then I pause…and say, 'And why would you want to make the bully happy?'

Their eyes do an odd wobble; they look flabbergasted and reply,

'I don't know, I didn't realise.' This is the beginning of power!

Tell your child: Your anger and fear make you an easy target; you give the bully power to continue. He doesn't need another target, unless you change or leave. Don't show your pain for the bully's gain.

Parents and kids activity

The big switch from pain to power
Energise the survival instinct

Parents and kids activity

Tell your child: Like every living being, you're born with a survival instinct. This basic, primitive sensor detects danger and protects you. It is also called a 'gut feeling' or the 'fight or flight instinct'. It creates the anger or fear to get us moving and do something to protect ourselves. It is normal, natural and necessary. It provides you with the biochemical, hormonal power to take action. When you confront danger or need to flee, you switch on your survival instinct. Maybe your survival instinct was blocked or something trained you to switch off when you could have been alert and active. There may be many reasons, such as you were bullied at home or you'd never had to deal with mean kids before. Regardless of whether the bullying is subtle or obvious, you need to take action to protect yourself and survive in the school jungle.

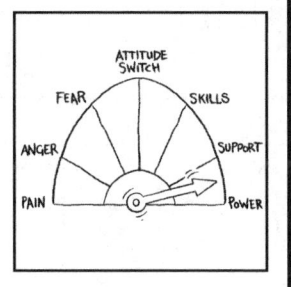

Kids activity

Write down occasions when you used your survival instinct. Here are some examples:

You smelt something burning and told your mum.

You checked your homework diary and found something you needed to do by tomorrow.

You checked the depth of the water before diving in.

Change direction

Allan was always small. He was teased in primary school but relied upon his older brother to confront the bully. When Allan began Year 9, a fat boy who was

repeating the year picked him up and threw him into the class rubbish bin every day for a week. Allan was very upset. The following week, Allan walked into the class and, instead of sitting in his usual seat, went straight to the rubbish bin and sat in it. Everyone in the class laughed. The bully was struck dumb but was forced to laugh with the rest of the class. Allan had stolen the bully's thunder. The bullying ended.

Parents and kids activity

Tell your child: Many children expect instant miracles when they ask for help. This could happen, but change usually comes from lots of hard work. The further you move away from your starting point, the greater the distance from your original path. So a tiny change in behaviour means a change in direction, which makes a big difference down the track. Reward yourself for any small changes of behaviour which prove you have changed direction.

Note: Adults working with children need to magnify and reinforce any positive change, and keep on magnifying, until the child sees and feels it. This creates his new direction.

Parents and kids activity

Try an instant mood flip

Tell your child: Imagine that you are feeling in an ordinary mood, and suddenly you receive some really great news, e.g. winning an overseas holiday; or very bad news, e.g. that someone you love is badly injured. Your mood changes instantaneously: your brain releases hormones which make you feel immediately different. Parents see children change moods when something good is about to happen. Children see angry parents turn polite the moment the phone rings or visitors arrive. Everyone can change mood very quickly when necessary. When you change your mood, you change your behaviour.

Change your mindset when bullies are close. Hide your anger and fear. Take away the bully's power by appearing cool and calm. And always inject yourself with some confidence.

Say to your child, 'If I gave you a million dollars, could you behave like a cool kid in front of a bully? How would you look and stand? What facial expression would you use and how would your voice sound?'

Parents and kids activity

Say, 'You can pretend.'

Now say, 'Tell me about a fantastic experience you have had or would like to have.'

Watch their behaviour. Every child will show some signs of looking more confident.

Respect the law of averages (probability)

Tell your child: Many children don't realise that there are many options to block bullying, and give up too quickly. Perhaps you don't realise that you or someone else could block the bullying once you find the right option.

Parents and kids activity

Kids activity

'Take a chance'

Children I have done this exercise with usually find it very encouraging.

- Toss a dice ten times.

- Record the number of sixes and ones.

- You may get one or more sixes and ones.

- Now repeat another 40 times.

- You will get around six to eight sixes and ones.

In a board game, everyone wants the six, which equals success, whereas the one is a bummer. The six represents something that blocks bullies, whereas the one is a learning experience or mistake. When you toss a dice many times, you throw some successes and some bummers. No-one achieves successes (sixes) without bummers (ones). The two go together – the more bummers or failures you have, the more successes you get. By the law of averages, something you do will stop the bully.

Activate your power

Parents and kids activity

Tell your child: Children who have been bullied often appear like doormats. They're so accustomed to bullies walking all over them that they look flattened and feel paralysed. If you are blocking bullies, you need to understand what power is, and use it. You will find that experiencing a surge of power is an addictive feeling. Learn how to use it respectfully, assertively and constructively.

Can you remember any moments when you felt a surge of power, e.g. when you first tied shoelaces/learnt to read/confronted parents/went somewhere alone/obtained a good school result/won a game/fixed something difficult? Think about when you've achieved something special. Do you remember the power surge? Can you create a power surge for blocking bullies, such as: look them in the eye and stand still?

What are three things you can do to feel powerful?

1. ....

2. ....

3. ....

Kids activity

Use anchors

Tell your child: Every boat requires powerful anchors to stop it drifting with the tide. People use emotional anchors to make them feel good, confident and empowered. Generally they are linked to something special. Some people use religious symbols as an anchor, others use their mobile phone, a toy or some jewellery. You can create your own anchors to give you a feeling of power. For example, when you block a mean kid, you could anchor your feeling of power with a smile. Then every time you see that child you could smile to unlock your power. You could anchor this powerful moment to an action (such as touching your ear) or an object (such as a toy).

Parents and kids activity

Parents and kids activity

Adult to child: 'Tell me what you felt inside when you achieve something important.'

Then say, 'What action or object can you use to remind you of that special feeling?'

Then reply, 'Whenever you need power, you can access that feeling by using your anchor.' Make sure you remind them about this from time to time.

Use feedback

The moment Jack got on the school bus everyone groaned. He was so fat that someone would end up getting squashed. He felt bullied.

Parents and kids activity

Tell your child: Every time you say or do something to another living being, you get a response. It can range from extremely subtle, such as a raised eyebrow or a stare, to the very obvious, such as a mean tease or a kick in the shins. The response is called *feedback*. You use feedback to identify nice and nasty people. If you don't listen to feedback, you may overlook the kids who are just having fun. Then you risk payback because they felt rejected by you. Or you could be bullied by mean kids and be blind to games which turn nasty.

In fact, you always need to make yourself safe. This includes stranger danger, risky physical situations, avoiding a dog attack and dealing with bullies. Feedback is your safety guide. It tells you how to use your survival skills to protect yourself and shows you what to do next. You need to check out everything to find out who is friendly or nasty. You need to observe the bully's behaviours – e.g. his eyes, face, body language, voice – and onlookers' reactions. Then check your gut feelings. Do you feel safe or not? Then take appropriate action, alone or with help.

An example of feedback is 'Pin the tail on the donkey', Blind Man's Bluff, or Marco Polo, a water game. You continue until you hear the right feedback, e.g. 'Very hot', which means you are in the right spot. You get your prize.

There are three types of feedback:

1. Positive – you feel comfortable, safe, happy.

2. Constructive – you can take action to help yourself.

Parents and kids activity

3. Destructive/Negative – you feel hurt, scared, threatened, angry.

Ask your child for examples of different types of feedback and show him how to categorise it into positive, constructive and destructive. You can begin with sibling talk.

Responding to feedback

Your child may be slow to hear the changes in your voice when you are tired of reminding him to do his chores, get ready for bed, or when he is annoying you by being rude, insensitive or difficult. Say: 'I feel… when you… and if you don't change your unacceptable behaviours, then as a consequence I will…'.

Similarly, your child may not realise when his behaviour is upsetting a sibling, grandparent or someone else, or when he is being unfriendly, lazy or inattentive to his friends.

Say: 'I didn't like it when you did… to… What can you do to behave with respect and friendliness?'

See Chapter 10 for more on feedback.

'Nobody bullied me!'

Sometimes a child I've been helping returns a few weeks later and tells me that she didn't practise because nobody bullied her. I feign surprise and say, 'It's a pity they didn't bully you because now we don't know which retorts work.' Then I say, 'Well, I've been too busy to go to the school and bribe the bullies to stop, did your parents bribe them?'

'No,' she laughs.

Then I ask the child, 'Why did the bullies stop?'

Eventually, she realises that the bullies changed because she changed her behaviours.

Find the smile

The really big switch begins when an unhappy child suddenly stops looking miserable and instead smiles. This may happen when she hears a funny retort. Sometimes I ask, 'Why are you smiling?' Words that seemed so painful half an hour ago now elicit a smile. She says, 'That's funny'.

While you are helping your child learn bully-blocking skills, look for the smile. It is essential feedback. It shows that your child feels positive and can block the bully. Let her know that she is smiling about blocking bullies!

Parents and kids activity

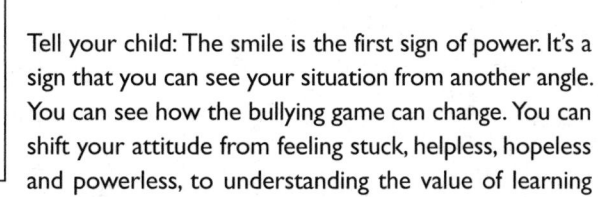

Tell your child: The smile is the first sign of power. It's a sign that you can see your situation from another angle. You can see how the bullying game can change. You can shift your attitude from feeling stuck, helpless, hopeless and powerless, to understanding the value of learning assertive skills and taking away the bully's power. At the unconscious level the smile shows that you like being assertive and you sense that it won't be hard.

Key points

- Trash faulty attitudes to change behaviour.
- Get rid of bad habits: don't let your child make the bully happy.
- Make the big switch from pain to power.

What to do

- Change your child's mindset to become positive.
- Identify feedback and use it to help your child protect himself.
- Activate your child's power.
- Find the smile.

6

How parents can help

Mary is an attractive, intelligent child aged eight years. She moved schools because she was being bullied. Her previous school, despite its high status and religious affiliations, ignored the bullying. She is shy, and seldom complained to her teacher, although her parents went to the school ten times in three years. Mary felt as though her 'insides were on fire'. Her parents moved her to a new, caring school. They soon discovered that she was so hurt by the previous bullying that she couldn't enjoy the friendly kids and safe environment at her new school, so they took her for counselling. They realised that they needed to change as well: they had to become more socially aware to help her reduce her shyness. They had to develop assertive skills and encourage her to use more eye contact, facial expression, a stronger voice – which they did. She is now enjoying her new school.

Children need exposure to some germs to build their physical resilience. Similarly, training them to deal with school bullies equips them for managing pushy friends, aggressive bosses, controlling partners and others. Bully blocking is a basic life survival skill. Conversely, once a child stops bullying others, he is more likely to attract respect, success and true friendships. And once children have the social confidence and skills to protect themselves, they can take risks, increase their social adventures and widen their social circle.

Although the school plays a significant role in reducing bullying, it must not be held totally accountable. Parents are ultimately responsible for teaching their children social survival skills.

Check your own feelings

Being the parent of a target or a bully is a very distressing experience. You may feel anger, fear, shame, confusion, frustration, embarrassment and powerlessness, according to whether your child is being targeted or is bullying others.

- You connect her experiences with those you experienced at her school, e.g. being excluded by a group of 'cliquey' parents.

- If you've experienced bullying at work, by a partner or elsewhere, painful memories may surface when your child is bullied. You recall your feelings of confusion, frustration, pain and powerlessness.

- If you recall being bullied at school, you probably didn't tell your parents. If you did tell them, they were either powerless or instructed you to 'walk away or thump them back.' Apart from the counsellor, most schools were ineffectual.

- You may blame yourself for not protecting your child or not teaching her social skills.

- You may feel frustrated when your child is labelled a bully, deny or blame others, even though unconsciously you are aware of the reasons. Perhaps you feel guilty because other difficult personal issues absorb your attention. If your child has been labelled a bully, intervene quickly so that she is not handicapped by this.

- Did you grow up in a passive, powerless, unempathic or authoritarian, physically or verbally abusive family?

- Do you have bad memories of being bullied? How did it affect you then and now? Did you get help? Release any pain (see Chapter 8) so that you can focus on your child, who needs your attention now. Share this with your child, so she feels less alone.

- Have you ever excluded, teased, denigrated, spread gossip, shouted at or manipulated someone else regularly? Unless you are a saint, you have probably inadvertently bullied others, e.g. siblings, partner, work colleagues or friends. Share this with your child.

- Obtain support and feedback from your partner, family and friends.

- Improve your own coping strategies: relax, de-stress (see Chapter 8), value yourself (see Chapter 10), improve your communication skills (see Chapter 11), and empower yourself (see Chapter 12).

- Establish support networks at school with staff and other parents. Join the parents' association, do voluntary work or see the counsellor.

- Are there any other personal or family difficulties at home? If you can't balance your stresses and strains while your child is suffering, obtain psychological help.

What's happening at home?

My mother is a very sweet old lady. All my life I've tried to avoid upsetting her because she has been through so much. I only learnt how to say 'No' at a recent family reunion. So it's not surprising that I found it hard to say 'No' to everyone else.

I allowed them to bully me.

As you have seen earlier, children learn how to show empathy and deal with conflict by communicating, caring and facing challenging issues within their family. This may happen when the family congregates around the dinner table and shares the ups and downs of the day or when family members share an activity together, e.g. washing dishes or cooking.

In many families the parenting patterns are based on outdated cultural traditions, their own parents' example, or are controlled by current factors such as the hectic pace of modern life, work obligations, social isolation, exhaustion, electronic gadgets, personality difficulties or marital issues. Sadly, the modern busy family schedule leaves little room for connecting and communicating (see Chapter 3).

Some parents provide a protected environment, so their children grow up oblivious to the jungle outside. Some parents manipulate, denigrate and bully. They use passive and aggressive behaviours, inconsistent boundaries and inappropriate ways to confront difficult situations.

When a child lacks or loses the opportunity to argue, negotiate or say 'No' to either parent, he can't confront a bully. Besides, if family members can't respect one another, you can't expect school peers to do so. Children learn from their families how to be targets, bullies or both. Regardless of the reasons, renovate your role modelling for your child and provide him with the confidence to cope, confront and continue.

Here are a few suggestions:

- Check the comfort level of banter/teasing at home. If it causes distress, reduce the denigration and replace it with respect.

- Demonstrate to your family your disapproval of all forms of bullying. Stop any bullying and deal firmly with any family members who do.

- Encourage your children to assist their siblings or others to block bullying at school.

- Provide a stable environment and don't split role models. A child can't become assertive when one parent is supportive while the other parent prohibits confrontation or can't cope with distressing information.

- Don't allow the goalposts to keep moving. Maintain firm behaviour boundaries for your children.

- Give consistent rewards for positive behaviours and consequences for disrespectful behaviours.

- Treat your child age-appropriately with regards to his responsibilities, privileges and restrictions, e.g. chores, social activities and travelling alone.

- Monitor your child's activities carefully, including his room, hobbies and schoolwork, and make sure that he doesn't misbehave and befriend children who do dodgy, dangerous deeds.

- Become empathic, resilient, friendly and respect others' rights in order to maintain positive role modelling.

- Respect and reinforce the school's actions when they are constructive.

Is the school target a home bully?

Targets can be bullies, and vice versa. Some targets have a bad day at school and then release their frustrations by bullying siblings and parents. Sometimes I ask a child, 'Something is wrong. You don't like being bullied at school, so why do you do it at home and hurt others?' I get a sheepish reply: 'I don't know.' Perhaps your child comes home looking distressed, so you inquire, 'What's wrong?' In a passive-aggressive way – which hides his true feelings – he explodes, 'Nothing!' He rejects your concern, runs out of the room and slams the door.

In such cases:

- Don't attack back or become defensive.

- Give empathy training to make him responsible for his behaviours.

- Tell him how you feel when he is mean, e.g. 'I feel...when you...'.

- Check his verbal and nonverbal feedback – this forces him to become totally accountable to you.

- If he cares about you and apologises, he's learning empathy.

- If he doesn't care about your feelings and doesn't absorb your message, repeat it until he does.

- Alternatively, give him a consequence to help him learn empathy, e.g. 'As you don't care how I feel, I won't give up my free time to take you to...' (see Chapter 11).

Discussing the problem with your child

A child of any age can share what she thinks and feels, provided she feels secure and safe. Parents need to find out from their child what has been happening, and involve her in dealing with bullying. Beware that if you barge into school 'on the warpath' and attack, your child will fear the repercussions and be less likely to confide in you in future.

The direct approach

The simplest way to find out if a child is being bullied is to ask directly, e.g. 'Is anyone being mean to you? Are they bullying you? What are they doing?' Then observe her body language when she replies. Does your child answer the question directly, e.g. 'Yes' or 'No'? If so, do the 'Whodunnit' exercise with your child.

Once you have established that your child is being bullied, fill out this questionnaire with her. It is essential to obtain the whole story – this is crucial for school meetings, and allows you to monitor any changes. It may also be useful later on to improve the school's legal accountability. Use a notebook, index cards (one per week) or a computer to maintain a record of the bullying until it ends.

The 'Whodunnit' exercise

Parents and kids activity

1. The bully:

- Boss bully 1...

  Bully 2...

  Bully 3...

  Bully 4...

  Bully 5...

  (Include her grade next to her name.)

- Teases, calls me names, says something as I walk past...

- Pushes, punches, hits, kicks, threatens, pinches, touches me in a mean manner...

- Leaves me out, talks behind my back, spreads nasty gossip, gives threatening looks, uses me, threatens me, breaks my belongings, sends mean text messages, emails and lies about me to other kids...

2. I think the bully:

- is fooling around and doesn't mean to upset me   yes/no

- enjoys hurting me   yes/no

- just follows the bully leader   yes/no

- is still my friend   yes/no

- used to be my friend   yes/no

- bullies other kids too   yes/no

- became a bully after our disagreement   yes/no

3. I am bullied:

- Every day...

- Once a week..

- Once a month...

- At the beginning of school year or term................................

- I have been bullied at these schools:...................................

  ....

- I have been bullied for......... years.

4. This is where I am bullied (draw a map):

- Home → walk/bicycle/car/bus/train/boat/tram → school

- School: classroom → office → library → hall → change rooms → lockers → toilets → sports→ oval → laneways → football field → swimming pool → yard → canteen.

- Local community: shopping mall, movies, playground, after-school activities e.g. tennis, swimming, football.

5. This is what I say and do when I am bullied:
   (e.g. 'I say the same thing back.' 'I pretend I didn't hear.' 'I don't want to lose my friends so I don't tell them how I feel.')

   ....

   ....

   ....

. The students who witnessed the bullying:

- While it was happening they...

- The students who tried to help me were.................................

- While it was happening my friends......................................

. I reported it to the school: when? where? how often?

- These teachers were helpful:..

- These teachers were unsympathetic: ....

- These teachers tried but weren't successful:...........................

8. What actions did the school take?

- Did it stop some or all of the bullying?.......................................

- Did it do nothing?..

- Did it make it worse?..

9. Who else is being bullied?..

10. What else is happening at school? e.g. your main teacher is away for a semester, there is a temporary principal, everyone is recovering from a school tragedy, etc.

....

....

The indirect approach

If your child won't discuss the problem, try this indirect approach.

Sometimes parents and teachers hear about the bullying from another source. When they confront the child, they may encounter denial, negation or minimisation of the bullying. It can sound like this: 'I am used to being teased' or 'I just try and forget it is happening' or 'I don't mind' or 'He started it'. Most children don't like upsetting their parents or involving teachers, so don't listen to the first layer of denial. Discuss with your child the dangers of being bullied and the importance of doing something constructive.

Be aware that children of all ages are exposed to nasty swear words at most primary and secondary schools: the worst words, e.g. the 'f' word, are used in Year One in the best private schools! Many children are too scared or embarrassed to tell adults about the toxic swear words they receive – 'How could I tell my parents that he told me to "get fucked" when I'm not allowed to swear at home?'

Question her: 'Has anyone said or done anything else that makes you feel very bad, but you are not sure if you are allowed to tell me?' Give your child permission to talk about these bad words, even though she is not normally allowed. Unless exposed, these words may continue to wound your child for years to come.

Ask your child:

'What are the words used to tease children at your school?'
'What are the nasty things children do to other children?'

'What do the other children do while it is happening?'
'What do you do?'
'Do the teachers know, and what do they do?'
'What is the most hurtful form of bullying?'

And then (after a pause):

'Has this ever happened to you?'
'How often does it happen in a day, a week or a month?'
'Where does it happen – class, corridor, yard, on the way to school?'
'What do your friends do?'
'Do they know how upset you are inside?'
'Does the school know you are very scared every day?'

You as social coach

We know that some shy children can blossom into social beings, while others remain socially inept or handicapped, more likely to bully or be bullied. The psychologist, school counsellor or a caring teacher can see a child for only a few hours each week. But you, as the parent, have far more time to coach your child and build his social and emotional resilience. You provide the early social learning environment for your children. This is later adapted and modified by other social experiences at school and elsewhere.

One day someone enterprising will create a social survival skills programme which can be directly installed into a child's brain. Meanwhile, help your child trash his negative beliefs and replace them with respectful, assertive, self-protective behaviours. All the skills in this book are practised every day, everywhere, by confident, popular children. If you don't believe me, then just check with your child how the sociable, popular kids would react in a similar situation.

Here are a few coaching tips:

- Apply flexibility to use the appropriate techniques in this book.

- Use assertive behaviours instead of passive or aggressive ones.

- Coach your children about the qualities required for true, caring friendships and assist them to create and maintain these friendships.

- Take an active role in encouraging social activities.

Now let's look at the key factors in social coaching.

Family time

Children need a social life at home in order to learn the skills for school. They require regular opportunities to develop these skills, e.g. family meals, picnics, barbecues, outings, holidays, playing games, cooking, gardening and sharing household chores. Provide opportunities for your children to share the ups and downs of their day, like 'show and tell' in class. Busy families could aim for at least two meals a week together around the table, free of any electronic 'blah blah'.

Family meetings

Like any voluntary or professional organisation, you need regular meetings to replace the contact lost by your hectic lifestyle and other factors. These family meetings discuss day-to-day business and reinforce your informal chats or discussions. You can model effective communication skills and problem-solving behaviours for your children.

- Meet regularly, e.g. once a week/fortnight, for 30–45 minutes.

- Everyone creates the rules for the proper conduct of the meeting.

- Elect, delegate, share or rotate the roles of agenda planner, chairperson and record keeper.

- Set a regular time when everyone is available and relaxed, e.g. on the weekend.

- Find a suitable location away from phones, computers, games and television.

- Discuss past and future activities, chores and perceptions.

- Negotiate fair rewards and disciplinary action.

- Use this time to obtain the family's support about dealing with bullying.

Bring workplace skills home

Most people who go to work receive some training to improve work relation-ships. The skills you learn at work can be used at home, e.g. how to deal with difficult people, assertiveness skills and conflict resolution. Similarly, the basic social survival skills in this book are used in training seminars – you can bring them back to work!

- Share your workplace experiences with your children (many haven't a clue what their parents do).

- Most likely you've dealt with difficult colleagues, clients, customers or bullies. Share your difficult experiences and any effective techniques.

Who's who

A child needs a variety of role models, including the appropriate male and female perspectives.

- Unless there is genuine danger from an abusive parent, most children need the support and assistance of both parents to deal with bullying. This also reduces overprotectiveness, counteracts sabotage and encourages assertiveness.

- Regular use of the phone, fax, Internet, mobile phone with temporary or permanent absentee parents is important.

- If your child has only one active parent, find other role models, e.g. a Scout leader or football coach for a boy, an older girl or female teacher for a girl.

Unstick secrets

If your child has been told to keep family secrets, this can sap the energy he needs to protect himself. Provide him with simple alternatives so that, if asked, he can say something brief and move on. Otherwise he is forced to remain silent, which will handicap his social life. He can't chat about everything and have fun, and can become lonely and attract bullying. Here are some sample responses:

- Marital problems: 'Mum and Dad treat each other like cat and dog.'

- Financial difficulties: 'We are on a very tight budget.'

- Alcohol, drug or gambling problems: 'They have a common-sense deficiency.'

The confidence con

Your child may say, 'When I have confidence, I will...'. Show them that confidence is not a goal, but a reward for confronting challenges. Like happiness, it comes in flashes and disappears the next time you begin another challenge. Children need to learn that confidence means accepting fear, pushing it aside, taking a risk and doing what they need to do until they feel successful. Discuss examples of how you or others they know built confidence and then faced another hurdle, e.g. learning a skill. You can use Chapter 11 to coach your child how to act with confidence.

Resilience training

Some parents want children to live in a cocoon of contentment (a virtual womb), but this only increases their vulnerability. Parents can't always protect their children from danger, so it's pointless providing a protected school environment without offering training in the 'jungle' rules. Children need to learn how to protect themselves from mean, difficult people wherever they are.

- Show your child(ren) that although bad things happen to nice people, it's how they cope, survive and move on that builds their emotional and social resilience.

- Encourage them to use assertive, not aggressive or passive, skills to confront, retort and negotiate at home and school.

- Remind them of the 'Old Choo Choo' train – it went, 'I think I can, I think I can', and so on. Explain how they have nothing to lose, as the situation can't get much worse. 'What is the worst thing that could happen if you try out an idea and it doesn't work?'

- Give them the courage to do things differently.

- Re-frame and offer encouragement if they experience failure, e.g. 'Better luck next time', 'Good on you for trying' or 'This works for me, do you want to give it a go?'

- Create a positive future: 'What would happen if you played with another group of kids who aren't nasty?' or 'Once you retort, don't be surprised if no-one bullies you and kids want to be your friend!'

- Enrol them in a martial-arts programme to learn confidence and self-protective skills.

Bribery works

If your child is finding change difficult, use positive reinforcement or bribery. Once he learns a new technique for a reward, show him that he can change. It's far wiser to utilise a little bribery or positive conditioning than to have a depressed, traumatised child!

- Make time for your child to tell you how he handled the bully today.

- Remind him that any change in his behaviour is better than doing nothing. It puts the bully on alert, and the game may turn against the bully.

- While he is training, don't discipline him for being more aggressive or cheeky. It's hard regulating feelings when he'd rather be angry and abusive!

- Find motivators, e.g. a chocolate bar, a game, an outing, points for a treat at the end of the week.

- Praise any successes.

- Demonstrate his value to you every day, e.g. loving notes, lunchbox treats, SMS messages.

Practice makes it better

Some children don't like change. If they protest, 'But that's not me!' you can reply, 'Well, who is it?' Everyone changes physically all the time, learns new skills and adapts to new situations. At first it feels odd, but as you learn something new you progress from ignorance and confusion to using it automatically and naturally.

- Help your child understand that he will still be the same person he was before he learnt how to tie shoelaces, play football or learn new computer games, and will be the same child once he learns how to deal with bullies, except he will feel better!

- Encourage your child to learn comfortable bully-blocking skills.

- Work out when and how often you can help your child practise.

- A tape recorder, a video recorder and/or a diary can be useful.

Nothing happened and nothing worked!

Most children don't recognise many good or bad things happening around them. If they tell you that nothing worked, don't believe them. No child enjoys being bullied, and will usually try different techniques to deal with the situation. Unfortunately, they don't always know exactly how to do it, nor do they always persist (see Chapter 5).

- Remind them about the law of averages. If they employ a variety of strategies and practise them, something has got to work.

- Look for any change or minuscule improvement in what they say or do, e.g. 'Only one kid bullied me today' or 'No-one teased me today'. Then re-frame, magnify, acknowledge and praise.

Healthy bodies make healthy minds

Bullying is a stressful game. Children need to be healthy to confront it. Many children who are bullied avoid the playground and find refuge in a library or computer room. They don't do enough exercise to remain healthy and to physically release their negative emotions. Some overdose on comfort food and put on weight, which will increase the bullying and decrease their self-esteem.

- Help the target develop a healthy lifestyle, which includes a balanced diet, sufficient sleep and daily exercise (minimum 30 minutes). This excludes school sport, where he may stand around doing little.

- Help the child who uses bullying behaviours to have a healthy diet, reduce sugar intake to lower his aggression, and use daily exercise to release frustration (minimum 45 minutes).

Electronic 'blah blah'

As mentioned in Chapter 3, electrical and electronic equipment has enriched our lives, but it can be abused. Some children are allowed unlimited television, computer/Internet/electronic game time. The research is clear: being hooked to an electronic screen can lead to depression, social isolation and loneliness. Unfortunately, this is where many shy children disappear. Electronic security blankets may replace valuable socialising time. Chatting on the Net will *never* replace face-to-face interaction, unless humans are genetically reprogrammed. Some children claim that they release their frustrations while playing computer games, but there is limited supporting evidence. They need to do something physical and verbal with someone who is real – otherwise their gut instinct can't function.

- Limit your child's electronic time to about one or two hours per day.

- Provide instructions on computer usage and check regularly to see what he is doing.

- Make sure he is not an electronic target or bully.

- Remind him that electronic bullying can be traced.

- If your child has problems, contact the service provider to block the mean kids, and tell the police, school, etc. (See also Chapter 12.)

Humour works

Humour lowers stress levels within the body, releases emotional pain and is extremely therapeutic. Humour allows your child to see the situation from a positive perspective and reduces the emotional tension between peers. When a child laughs, he breathes in more oxygen, which neutralises his fear and anger. Encourage your child to use humour more often, have fun and fool around. Then he will attract more friends.

- Make sure he doesn't play the fool to compensate for a lack of friendship skills.

- Suggest he becomes a straight or funny comedian.

- Encourage him to bring a funny story or joke to school regularly.

- Humour can motivate a target or bully to change without making them defensive.

- Always look for the smile and enjoy your child's positive attitude as it emerges.

- Magnify and reinforce successful behaviours with fun, humorous comments, poems and re-frames.

RE-FRAME, DON'T BLAME
'The bully is training you how to block bullies.'
'The bully is reminding you to improve your social skills.'
'It's good to be on top, just make sure you're not on a see-saw.'
'You've only been mean once today.'
'The poor bully, your talents remind him of how successful you will become.'
'It's okay to be sensitive but just reduce the volume.'

CREATE FUN INTERPRETATIONS
'How many times did you raise your right eyebrow/fart at them today?'
'Tell us today's news – what's on the bully bulletin today?'
'Bullies are like sharks. Did you join their feeding frenzy today?'

USE HUMOUR
'Today a rooster, tomorrow a feather duster.'
'Today's bull is next week's barbecue.'
'I saw the bully today – she has a stunning lack of charisma.'

BECOME POLITICALLY CORRECT
Don't say someone is dumb, call them 'aesthetically challenged'.
If friends won't listen, call them 'hearing impaired'.
If they call your son a 'girl', he can tell them to be 'gender specific'.

CARTOONS/MOVIES
Show them funny cartoons that are relevant, e.g. The Simpsons, or movies, e.g. Steve Martin in Roxanne. Point out funny examples on television or something you have heard that gives them good ideas on how to deal with bullying, such as clever retorts.

Parents' action plan – coaching guidelines

Although it is very painful dealing with bullying, you need to develop a sensible set of strategies to help your child. Your constructive approach will serve as an effective piece of role modelling for them to follow, and will help them develop resilience.

Hot tips

What's hot	*What's not*
Get the big picture	Don't automatically blame others
Be empathic	Don't overprotect your child
Maintain behaviour boundaries	Don't be inconsistent
Encourage resilience	Don't allow them to deny problems
Be positive and optimistic	
Choose a variety of options	Don't remain angry and powerless
Persistence is the key	Don't rely solely on the school
Look for the smile	Don't try then give up easily
	Don't do nothing

If your child is a bully

*One mother was sick and tired of her son being a bully.
With the school's support, she supervised him everywhere – in class
and in the yard at school. After a day he vowed never to bully again.*

Although some parents believe it is acceptable to bully or stand up and fight, deep down most parents are ashamed that their child has to abuse his power to remain popular. Thus they deny and make excuses. But bullying boomerangs back on bullies – they suffer too. You don't want your child to have a bad life just because he bullies. He has a right to a normal life.

Find out why your child is bullying. Is he copying everyone else in his group, or is it due to other stressors? Assess your family role models and get help to change. Encourage your child to become nicer, more assertive and constructive so that he can enjoy positive relationships and run less risk of being sabotaged. Then review the action taken. If it worked, celebrate. If not, discuss other ways to stop his bullying behaviours.

Here are a few suggestions:

- Don't blame your child – everyone bosses and bullies at times.

- Find out what your child did and why. He may feel powerless, under pressure to conform, or maybe project his difficulties.

- Check if there is something else stressing him that requires your attention.

- Alter your role models, become consistent and respectful.

- Spend positive time with your children to build their self-esteem, and reward positive behaviours.

- Teach them how to show empathy and respect.

- Monitor their friendships, encourage them to avoid mates who bully.

- Structure their free time with lots of activities, e.g. chores, hobbies.

- Demonstrate the difference between aggressive, passive and assertive behaviours.

- Send them to a martial-arts course to control their aggression.

- Encourage their teacher to keep them busy and reward their efforts.

- Demonstrate that bullying is bad and an apology is necessary.

- Children require fair, firm rules. Describe the consequences if they bully, and implement them, e.g. remove television/ computer/computer games/mobile phone; ground them; have them do volunteer work, donate to charity, and research bullying.

- Collaborate with the school and obtain regular feedback to help them improve.

- If your child's friends are bullies, warn your child and report them a few weeks later to the school.

- Obtain professional help for you, your child and your family.

If your child is provoking the bully

Some children try to play with other children but are rejected because their social skills are poor and they don't blend in. Their frustration can lead to attention-seeking behaviours which irritate and provoke other kids to bully. Some become so angry and hurt once excluded or bullied that they retaliate, provoke and fight back to protect themselves from feeling powerless. But they always lose. Unfortunately, if the school witnesses these retaliatory behaviours, they label the child a bully! If you just defend your child, you are wasting time. Find out what happened. Then you can recommend suitable options which help him to be accepted socially and find a nice bunch of mates.

Safety first

Although you may expect the type of justice portrayed on television, your first priority is to make your child safe. Look for the symptoms that identify your child as a target or a bully. You can't expect a busy school to notice everything. Then alert the school if she is unhappy, provided the school tries to handle it responsibly. Don't make the situation worse by doing nothing for months, by challenging the bully or her parents, by trusting a school that exacerbates the problem, or by denying your child therapy while suing the school.

Many children are so scared, angry or hurt that they lose sight of the bigger picture. They become stuck blaming others, giving up hope, or feeling terrified that the situation will deteriorate once reported. Sadly, this can happen. Then say to your child, 'I am concerned, but I will give you about three or four weeks to resolve this. If the bullying hasn't stopped by then, I will contact the school and get help. I don't want you to suffer any longer.'

Then do what is possible to show her your support and guarantee her safety, e.g. 'If the situation gets worse, I will consult the principal, the board, the police, a lawyer or the media. If it still doesn't improve, I can move you to another school or provide home schooling. I will keep going until the bullying stops. You need to trust me.' Make sure that you keep your word – you need to persist until she feels safe at school. Don't abandon your responsibilities by relying on her school to do the right thing. If it fails, she will feel abandoned by everyone. Eventually, you can empower your child to learn the appropriate skills to protect herself from any bully.

Report time – to tell or not to tell?

Many children are hesitant or scared to tell their parents and teachers about the bullying. And they are correct, it can get worse. So what do you do if they beg you to do nothing and insist that you don't inform the school, their other parent or siblings? Don't allow your child to imprison you in a code of silence. Clearly, she is ashamed or scared that things will deteriorate. But be on guard: secretiveness can breed violence. Besides, it may already be a real problem, and it won't improve unless something is done.

If your child fears publicity, tell her that most children know the bullies and targets. Besides, bullies know that if the school is unaware, it can't intervene, and they are free to commit further injury. If your child implores you to do nothing, tell her that you will teach her bully-blocking skills. Tell her that if nothing improves within three to four weeks, you will approach the school, as it would be irresponsible to allow your child to suffer, now or later. If your child is still terrified that the situation will deteriorate if you report, then guarantee her safety, e.g. 'I will protect you in this situation'. And make sure you keep your promise.

Remain calm and confident

- Encourage your child to report the bullying incidents to you.

- Listen carefully, be empathic, validate her experience.

- Provide unconditional support, feedback and care.

- Don't blame, criticise or devalue her.

- Remain calm and express your confidence that something constructive can be done.

- Plan your action.

Get the big picture

- Chat with your child about what has been happening and how she feels about being bullied or blamed.

- Encourage your child to work out why the bully selected her (e.g. jealousy), and how she makes a bully happy (e.g. looking upset).

- Find out why she is bullying (e.g. 'She is annoying us') and how she does it (e.g. 'We push her around').

- Determine whether she bullies or is being bullied by playmates, annoying kids or enemies.

Do your research and keep records

- Record every incident, including dates, photos of bruises, cuts, torn clothing, damage to belongings, other written or recorded material and any communication with the school.

- Encourage your child to keep her own Bullying Diary, to assess her improvement (see the 'Whodunnit' exercise).

- You'll be surprised what you can learn from siblings, relatives and friends. Use this information to coach your child.

- Look for a bullying pattern, e.g. at the beginning of term, during friendship difficulties or marital conflict, or following her absence due to holidays or ill health.

Use common sense

Obtain feedback about your child's behaviours when you're not around. This is a very emotional time for everyone, so you need to think through the issues carefully. Words said in the heat of the moment cannot be unsaid. Aim for flexibility and use what works. If your child has a single bully, it's simple to teach her retorts or social skills. But when your child is bullied by a gang of thugs or a bunch of 'bitches', it is an impossible challenge for just you and your child to manage – the school then needs to step in.

Sensible ideas for your child

- Provide your child with options, e.g. play with other students, avoid the bullies, visit her locker at other times.

- Instruct her to be on the alert, e.g. around narrow laneways, sports areas, at the end of recess.

- Encourage your child to find safe places at school, e.g. near friends or teachers.

- Instruct her to avoid risky places where bullying occurs, e.g. lockers, playground.

- Help her change her routines, e.g. find another route to class.

- Tell her to be wary travelling to and from school and at local public places, e.g. shopping centres, discos.

- Show her how to blend in and avoid unwanted, stressful attention by dressing and behaving like others, e.g. avoid unusual clothing and hairstyles, and don't boast.

- Tell her to hide items a bully can use, not to lend items or bring items a bully can steal, e.g. cash.

Don't sabotage

After I practised some great retorts with Sam, he didn't use them. He was bullied for another week because his mother didn't approve of the retorts, even though they were his choice, not mine. After our session, she realised that she had to allow him to choose what made him feel safe. In being overprotective, she was actually removing his initiative and power.

- Don't inhibit, restrict or sabotage your child, or condone the 'slow-moving school'.

- Some children resolve bullying by saying and doing things adults wouldn't dare do!

- Plan your action by collaborating with your child and her school.

- If your child is bullying, don't deny it – obtain the facts and professional assistance.

How do you assess progress?

There are two ways to assess a child's progress:

1. Her behaviours

- She looks happier and less stressed, has relaxed facial muscles (check cheeks, lips and eyes).

- Her feedback is positive, e.g. 'Nobody teased me this week', 'Everything's alright', 'Kids are nice to me'.

- What she does, e.g. comes home happy from school, mentions new friends, is keen to attend school, does her homework, has fewer tummy aches, etc.

2. Comments and actions by other people

- Other children wanting to be friends with your child, e.g. phoning at home, making new social arrangements, or your child suddenly sharing new stable friendships.

- Positive feedback from family, friends or the school.

Make sure that you use the feedback to boost her confidence, provide support and give her more ideas.

Dealing with your child's school

Bullying is a symptom of dysfunctional systems. It is important to collaborate where appropriate with your child's school, and be aware that he may have more resources and restrictions than you realise.

Understand the school's role

Schools need to be caring, responsible and sensitive to the needs of vulnerable students. If they have a firm policy of mutual respect, commitment and consistent programmes, there is less likelihood of institutionalised bullying (see Chapter 3). Some schools take bullying seriously: they acknowledge its toxic impact on morale, enrolments, staff, students, parents and the local community. Their actions indicate their constant focus on reducing it. Many schools pay lip-service to their policies but their actions are minimal. Hopefully, law suits, media attention, angry parents and financial difficulties will force insensitive or irresponsible schools to acknowledge their duty of care and respect everyone.

Dealing with bullying is a collaborative process. You can't expect a traumatised child to confront bullies, a bully to behave well in a bullying culture, or the school to function alone. Schools need to respect parents' rights to be involved, and parents need to understand the school's role and limitations.

Checklist

- Find the designated person at school who is supportive, communicates regularly and takes action, e.g. your child's teacher, counsellor, coordinator or principal.

- Make an appointment, and arrange simple, regular communication, e.g. phone, email, face-to-face meetings.

- Try to organise at least one meeting at school with your partner. If separated, either meet the teacher together or separately.

- Bring along your Bullying Diary, record the discussion and intended action. Plot any constructive or negative changes.

- Obtain copies of the school bullying policy and programmes, and discipline and welfare policies.

- Compare the general steps taken by the school to reduce bullying and the specific steps they will take to protect your child.

- Provide them with relevant background material about your child and family, provided confidentiality is respected and the information won't be used against you or your child.

- Keep them informed of any setbacks or improvements.

- If nothing is working and the school can't help, consult a doctor, a psychologist or a professional health or welfare agency that can liaise with the school.

- If there is no change after a term, consider other options, e.g. changing classes or schools.

- Before class lists are organised for the next grade, consult your child and the school about the wisdom of placing your child in another class with a former bully.

School rules for parents

- Bullying is the joint responsibility of the school, teachers, students and parents – not one person.

- A parent's role is to collaborate closely with the school to obtain maximum benefit for the child.

- Most schools lack the resources to reduce and eradicate bullying.

- Schools, like huge ships, take time to change course. Give them a 'fair go' – a few weeks to take action – and then renew contact.

- Beware of a school that fobs you off or makes a token effort.

- Respect the school staff. Don't automatically blame, threaten or make inappropriate demands. The teacher may be unaware, unskilled or may have heard other versions of the bullying. If you 'go on the warpath' to the school, threaten staff or other students, this will embarrass your child further. Then your child may be scared to tell you the whole story, or even any details at all, in future.

- Beware that your child may be a bully magnet or a trainee sociopath.

- Go higher and consult the principal, school governing body, state Department of Education, a lawyer, the police, etc.

- Don't feel guilty about making a fuss about bullying – you may be helping other children as well as your own.

Your experience is not unique

Jocelyn felt unsupported by her daughter's school. She planned to spend a few weeks working with her daughter to build her bully-blocking strategies. She also knew that other parents were unhappy. If nothing changed, she planned to send them a questionnaire. She would use the feedback to pressure the school to take action or contact the media. However, the school was very distressed by the bullying and took action.

It's nice to know that you are not alone and can meet with other parents whose children are being bullied. Besides, schools are more open to feedback from a bunch of parents than from just one. However, regardless of whether your child is being bullied by a friend or enemy, don't confront him or his parents. Like you, most parents reject criticism of their child and retaliate. A pleasant chat can deteriorate into an impasse, escalate into a parent brawl, or your child will be bullied for 'dobbing'. It's the school's responsibility to confront the bully's parents. In other words, don't bully others to protect your child.

Legal 'bullying'

Although schools have a legal and moral duty to provide a safe learning environment for students, if the school fails to protect the child and you want justice or validation, there are options:

- Consult the police, who can take an active role at school and warn students and families.

- Go to court for a restraining/intervention order to stop the bully coming near the target.

- Investigate your legal option to sue the school (or the state), staff and/or bully. This is a last resort, as schools generally have greater financial resources than parents to fight a case. And this does not enable the target to develop bully-blocking skills or heal his trauma.

- When bullies are treated unfairly they may be able to take action, e.g. under the laws of natural justice (on the grounds of procedural unfairness).

- Report to a human rights organisation or a member of parliament.

The media can help

No school desires negative publicity about their bullying problem. The threat of publicity may motivate them to become proactive and tackle bullying. Make sure that you obtain all the facts, e.g. compile a survey with other parents. If the school still refuses to confront the problem, despite recent evidence, then consider media action. Design a press release and find someone who can communicate effectively with the media.

Warning: Do not rush into this lightly. Staff will feel threatened and powerless. They may retaliate towards your child, no matter how respectfully the matter is handled. If this happens, be prepared to remove your child from the school.

Children with a disability

Angie has chronic fatigue syndrome, which has psychological and physical symptoms. This confuses her peers and teachers: sometimes she looks very well, and then she is sick for days. For the past six years students and teachers have said, 'You aren't sick, you're just faking.' She can instruct the bully: 'Come back at the same time tomorrow to discuss my chronic fatigue syndrome'.

Nina has an attention deficit disorder. Her classmates know that she takes medication to control her behaviour. They say things like, 'You're stupid for taking medicine'. She retorts: 'If I didn't take it, I'd be nuts, so I'd rather be stupid than nuts'.

Parents who have a child with a difficulty such as a physical handicap, a health problem or an educational problem tend to be overprotective in order to compensate and provide the extra support their child requires. This may increase their child's likelihood of being bullied. Parents become so accustomed to a child's difficulties that they can develop blind spots. They need to be aware of the impact of the difficulty on their child's life and on the remainder of the family, then make the appropriate adjustments.

- If your child has a physical condition – bad scarring, a cranio-facial deformity or a problem like eczema – then enhance his appearance (wearing cosmetics and trendy clothing) and his social skills (being friendly, developing hobbies to make them interesting).

- If your child has a medical condition, such as a kidney disease, cancer, scoliosis, attention deficit disorder, chronic fatigue syndrome, an obsessive-compulsive disorder, diabetes or facial-cranial difficulties, provide a short leaflet for curious peers and teachers explaining his condition (to be handed out every year).

- Practise 'question and answer' or role-play sessions before a return to school to reduce his anxiety about being teased.

Professional referral

Michael, aged 11, was a provocative target. His self-esteem was poor due to his mother's prolonged postnatal depression. Consequently, he was bullied and he bullied back. After the first few counselling sessions, the bullying had almost

*ceased. By the sixth session he was a much happier boy. His school report said,
'Throughout this year it has been incredible to see Michael flourish into a mag-
nificent young man.'*

I once saw a child who had been bullied for six years. The school tried to refer
him to a psychologist, but his parents didn't want to draw attention to the
bullying. They thought it would mean he had a problem (when he had one
already), would make it worse (but they did, by doing nothing) and he would feel
stigmatised (he did already). Although he'd suffered for years, treatment took just
six sessions! But even so, don't wait: the longer you wait, the longer it may take for
a therapist to help your child and teach her coping strategies. There is also
another risk: the scars may not be evident, but may lie dormant and have a more
destructive impact later on.

Some common concerns

Are you:

- scared the problem will be exacerbated?

- frightened to battle your child to get help when she refuses?

- being bullied by your child to do nothing?

Do you:

- fear it will reflect badly on you as a parent?

- believe the school has the problem, not your child?

- prefer to sue and punish than treat and empower your child?

- do nothing and hope your child stops being a target/bully?

- allow your child to be bullied for years before obtaining professional
  help?

- fear that your role modelling trains your child to remain a
  target/bully?

- disregard medical evidence that bullying can affect children forever?

- not believe in psychology and deny evidence-based professional
  practice?

- think your partner won't see the value in going, so you don't suggest it?

- not want to pay for a happier, healthier child?

- not want to shop around for a skilled therapist?

- come once and then cancel because your child found the experience too painful, was worried she'd exacerbated the bullying, and the therapist wanted your child to confront her pain and make some changes?

Trained counsellors spend many years studying the theory and practice of dealing with school bullying. They have all sorts of skills and aids; they use video cameras and games to teach children new skills. If you aren't able to help your child after reading this book, then investigate having between four and eight sessions of skilled counselling for your child. She should then be able to progress from feeling powerless towards enjoying life more.

Referral for help outside school

Although most children can be helped by a school-based counsellor, some will require an external referral. This reduces stigma, respects family privacy and reduces any defensiveness for the target, bully and their families. Children are less threatened in a non-school environment. They may be more likely to commit to learning new skills. Besides, the logistics of organising appointments, transport, babysitters and fees demonstrates to children that their parents are serious about blocking bullying.

How are you currently doing with all of the strategies discussed in this chapter? If you are already implementing many or most of them, well done – your child will soon be showing the benefits of your good work. However, if most of them are new to you, you need to have a good think about how they can apply to your family, and start implementing them.

Moving school

When all else fails, move schools when:

- the school is not safe

- it is not comfortable or the most suitable

- the school has blind spots: children and/or teachers have difficulty adjusting to a reformed target or bully, or

- a fresh start is needed: some children need a new school where they are not affected by their former reputation or the local grapevine.

A few things to consider

- *Timing*: From an educational perspective, it is better to move children at the end of a school year. But if the situation is bad, move them any time. The damage associated with remaining in a toxic school is worse than moving to another school mid-year.

- *Check out the new school*: Although all schools have bullying stories, find a caring school with a good discipline policy and effective anti-bullying practices. There is no major difference between coeducational or single-sex, small or large schools. Before selecting a new school, your child should spend time checking it out. Try to obtain feedback from other parents, consult your psychologist or an educational consultant, then ultimately trust your gut feelings in choosing the next school.

- *Chart the gossip flow*: Students on public transport and at local shopping centres facilitate the gossip between schools. It is pointless for your child to begin at a school where his reputation has preceded him. Your child may have to travel further to avoid it (like country children, who travel for hours to school and back).

- *Get help to begin again*: Although some children move to a school with no bullying, they may require professional psychological help to repair the damage, rebuild their self-esteem, learn self-protective techniques and make a successful transition into the new school. If they haven't learnt bully-blocking skills, a bully at the new school may want target practice.

- *'Why did you leave your last school?'* Oddly enough, an honest reply often stops further comment, e.g. 'I became tired of all the thugs/bitches' or 'The kids weren't very nice'. It may even encourage sympathetic children to be friendly. Besides, some kids will have heard through the gossip grapevine about that school already.

Alternatively, help your child provide a reasonable story, e.g. 'My parents wanted me to go to a school where my educational needs were being met' or 'I don't know, my parents decided'.

- *Correspondence schools/home schooling:* Some children who have been badly bullied avoid school. Although children can learn by correspondence, they lack regular exposure to other children. They won't learn how to communicate and protect themselves in difficult situations. Besides, this reinforces their self-image as a social failure, and handicaps their future. Home schooling may be appropriate for a brief period, provided the child is integrated into a normal school as soon as possible. If a parent has no other choice, he or she needs to structure a variety of normal, sustained, social, peer-group experiences for the child to replace what he is missing from school, e.g. a part-time job, team sports, martial arts, drama, voluntary work.

- *Boarding schools:* Bullying often thrives in boarding schools, which may have traditions of cyclical violence. Children are under threat of being bullied for 24 hours a day, compared to six hours a day at a day school, so the potential for damage is far greater. Unlike the day student, who can retreat back home to caring families, the boarder may be isolated from support. Parents should match their children to an appropriate boarding school. If unsafe, consider these options: change schools, become a day student (with private board), seek some dispute resolution and professional psychological help.

Key points

- Empower your children to learn the appropriate skills to protect themselves from any bully.
- It's painful being the parent of a target or a bully – find out if your child is a target or a bully or both.
- Understand your child's story; help him or her take action.
- Don't rely on the school to eradicate bullying.

What to do

- Renovate your parenting patterns to help your child.
- Help your child describe his or her bullying experiences.
- Coach your child in social survival skills.
- Keep a record.
- Collaborate with the school while respecting school rules.
- Consult a psychologist.
- If all else fails, give your child a fresh start.

7

What schools can do

The school prided itself on its level of education, superior teaching and values, but it was ignorant of the toxic impact of bullying, regarding it as part of school life. The school avoided anti-bullying programmes, which could generate unwelcome gossip, but was then confronted with a lawsuit. It hated the publicity and the legal costs, but it did absorb the message: a child's life had been threatened. The school developed policies and programmes. Despite being vigilant, bullying still occurs, but the school now intervenes with respect and everyone is treated fairly. The kids know that the bullying will be stopped. Not surprisingly, the school is now very popular, as parents seek a safe school for their children.

Every child has the right to feel safe at school. Thus, although schools should become bully-free zones, this is totally unrealistic. Firstly, the lack of knowledge, skills and resources to plan, implement and monitor bully-free programmes means that few professionals can bullyproof a school and reduce all forms of bullying, especially the subtle types. Current research demonstrates that most primary schools reduce bullying by 15 percent and secondary schools by 12 percent. Although Dan Olveus in Norway can reduce bullying by 42+ percent in some Norwegian and American schools, most schools don't have his commitment, time and resources. Besides, most schools don't involve parents, the bystanders, the peer group and teachers who need to alter their attitudes and actions to support anti-bullying programmes.

Secondly, schools are excellent environments for children to develop the basic life skills of emotional and social resilience. Once a child leaves school for the day or for good, bullies can still be encountered. The research into workplace bullying indicates that more than 15 percent of employees are seriously bullied at work, and many suffer devastating injuries. So bully-blocking skills can be very useful later on.

Thirdly, many schools are riddled with different types of bullying, from teacher to student, parent to teacher, student to teacher, teacher to teacher and so on. When parents complain, the school lawyers usually deny and bully back. In an Australian study, about 50 percent of teachers were bullied – usually by colleagues, but also by parents and students. It is futile to reduce school bullying for students while exposing them to other bullying role models. This will sabotage anti-bullying programmes.

In Chapter 3 we discussed three types of schools: those that deny – 'We don't have bullying here'; those that pretend, with pseudo-attempts – 'We have an anti-bullying policy'; and those that take genuine action to reduce bullying – 'We will take consistent action'. While schools must meet their ethical and legal obligations to reduce bullying (see below), you need to investigate what the school can achieve given its limitations. Be aware that reducing bullying will take a few years; it can't happen overnight. Then undertake the best course of action.

The school's ethical and legal obligations

Schools need to view bullying as an abuse of the human rights of the target, bully, onlookers, parents and teachers. They have a responsibility to handle all forms of violence as it is dealt with in their community. Ideally, schools need to regard bullying as a symptom of dysfunction, a relationship breakdown that requires respectful resolution (i.e. a win-win situation). Unfortunately, many schools reflect the broader society in adopting an adversarial approach whereby someone wins and someone loses.

Although human rights and ethical values could guide schools in establishing anti-bullying policies, in reality many schools are influenced by risk management issues, legal perspectives, police action or the media attention attached to suicides, murders and successful legal outcomes. These factors have, however, led to the establishment of state and national anti-bullying legislation or legal guidelines.

The predicament for every school is how to balance its cultural beliefs, ethical and legal responsibility towards eliminating bullying with its financial and staffing resources and the priority it allocates to a bully-free environment.

However, when schools are run effectively and each member of the school community is respected, involved and validated, bullying will reduce.

Schools can create safe, empowering environments for all children to learn and staff to work, including those who are different. The key messages are commitment, collaboration and consequences. Success depends upon a whole-school approach, mutual respect and a willingness to work together over a long period of time to obtain positive results. The major pitfalls are denial, inaction, injustice and a magical belief in the latest anti-bullying trend without an effective support framework.

This chapter provides a brief simple overview of how schools can deal with bullying. There are some excellent school-based programmes for those who require greater detail (see the 'Resources' section). Many individual schools have success stories. I would recommend that every teacher reading this book do further research.

> It was not one, single, ingenious thing that made the great difference, but the sum of many small moves. (The principal, Gran School, Norway)

Strategies to reduce school bullying

As you have seen, there is no 'one-size-fits-all' approach to reducing school bullying. This is a rough guide to the important steps to take. Each school needs to work out what is most effective for its particular school community.

1. Develop a committed whole-school policy

The best way to stop bullying is to accept that it exists, just like weeds and cobwebs. Every school needs to establish an appropriate anti-bullying, whole-school philosophy which is supported by an active, consistent prevention policy. This should include a code of conduct, protocol or guidelines for each school member, clearly defined actions (e.g. cyber bullying) and appropriate consequences. Ideally, the whole local community should be involved in this process, e.g. council, police, media.

Some schools prefer to embed bullying in a wider framework such as wellbeing or resilience. Others feel uncomfortable with an 'anti-bullying policy'. However, they must include the word 'bullying' in their policies, whether it is anti-harassment, welfare or discipline or any other policy – otherwise the true message will be lost.

- *Whole school* – The principal, students, parents and teachers, affiliated associations and local school district governing boards must be involved in making, maintaining and monitoring the school policy. The policies need to be comprehensive and deal with bullying at all levels, not just a problem class, and must include all forms of bullying, e.g. mobile phone and Internet bullying.

- *Culture change* – Good intentions are futile unless the school is truly committed to creating a peaceful environment and making the whole-school anti-bullying policies operational. This means that mutual respect is valued more highly than bullying, and that this is reflected in the common, everyday language.

- *Collaboration* – The school needs a collaborative approach to create a safe environment. Everyone who is actively associated with the school – including teachers, parents, students, targets, bullies, school board and local districts – needs to be involved and accountable for their role in reducing or preventing bullying. This includes everyone else connected to the school community, such as canteen workers, local shopkeepers, bus drivers and pedestrian crossing personnel.

2. Establish a task force

Schools have a fluctuating population. Delegating the task of 'dealing with bullying' to an excellent, caring staff member who may leave is unreliable. Schools need to establish a combined committee or task force representing every group associated with the school, e.g. students, teachers, parents, support staff, administrators and community members. It should include the counsellor and welfare staff, i.e. a school-based or visiting psychologist, social worker, chaplain, student welfare coordinator and pastoral care person.

- The task force members may vary from year to year but their purpose is ongoing and focused on reducing bullying.

- They could explore the extent and severity of bullying, use focus groups, consult colleagues and experts, investigate suitable options, research other successful programmes, select a variety of curriculum material, and help develop programmes.

- They should organise a support network so that the programmes are not implemented in isolation and fail.

- They need to monitor the policies and programmes annually. When appropriate, they can introduce new material and discard what is ineffective.

3. Investigate the bullying

Ideally, a target should feel safe and secure to report the bullying and relate her story, without fear of repercussions. Targets should expect a fair investigation followed by some form of resolution. Unfortunately, many children are too scared to report bullying, or they deny its impact once discovered. And its prevalence can vary from year to year. Schools need to realise that a child's perception of a single bullying incident may be as traumatic as it would be for many incidents, regardless of it being a minor tease or a vicious assault. The child who has one bully may require a different approach to the child confronting a gang. The school cannot plan, educate, initiate action or monitor programmes to reduce bullying without this information. Schools need to:

- investigate all types of bullying, both subtle and obvious, to assess the extent of the problem

- discover the game players, the patterns, types, frequency, severity and location of the bullying

- assess whether any action taken is successful or not and why

- establish who needs to be involved, e.g. parents, other students, staff, principal

- find the underlying dysfunctions within the school system that foster bullying

- choose and implement a validated school survey or design their own. Some may suit the school better than others. Surveys increase general awareness about bullying. See the 'Resources' section for some suggestions

- investigate other means of reporting bullying which guarantee confidentiality, e.g. random secret ballots conducted in class, a bully box where students can post a note, a phone/email connection in the library to a neutral source such as a designated staff member

- beware of bully surveys or other methods which students can manipulate to wrongly accuse someone, and

- maintain accurate records of detentions, suspensions, absenteeism, bullying incidents, sickness, children leaving school, lower academic results and other events which indicate bullying.

4. Develop public relations

Advertising has proved again and again that the more often the media informs people that something is good or bad, the more likely they are to change their behaviours. This has been successfully applied to driving more slowly and without alcohol, to reducing smoking and domestic violence. The school needs to regularly inform students, parents, staff and the local community that bullying is bad and that perpetrators risk penalties. They need to publicise designated support staff, as primary-school parents generally know whom to approach, whereas high-school parents are less informed. There are many ways a school can undertake publicity. These include:

- annual contracts, pamphlets, student diaries, newsletters, websites, intranet, email and phone text messages

- lectures/seminars, school assemblies, the public praising of 'acts of kindness'

- stickers, buttons, friendship bracelets, magnets, school posters (this could become a yearly competition)

- involving popular, well-known identities such as famous pop stars, sportspeople, actors, patrons and popular students to relay the anti-bullying message

- training in mediation and restorative justice, and

- conducting surveys that spread the anti-bullying message along the school community grapevine.

5. Enhance educational programmes

Some schools have excellent evidence-based, comprehensive programmes, others have limited programmes, and most have none. In general, schools need to timetable ongoing programmes to address the needs of the 5–16 years age group.

- In primary school, the focus should be classroom-based, so that the grade teacher can continually reinforce anti-bullying and pro-social messages.

- In high school, the teachers can integrate bullying into their subject, e.g. personal development, psychology, sports, drama, legal studies, health, statistics, religion, human rights and literature.

- Schools can have a theme for the year, e.g. discussing books, newspaper articles, films and television shows associated with bullying.

- There are some excellent evidence-based, comprehensive programmes available that can be integrated into general programmes which promote social and emotional resilience and reduce violence. See the 'Resources' section for listings of both types of programme.

- Alternatively, they can be embedded within general programmes about assertiveness training, communication skills, self-esteem and team building – again, see 'Resources'.

6. Train students, staff and parents

The school that is serious about reducing bullying needs to develop ongoing training programmes for students, staff, principal, school board and parents. Although some schools prefer to use their own staff to save funds and reduce publicity, it is wiser to use a regular combination of school-based staff and external experts for training.

School-based training professionals:

- need to research bullying and attend regular external training programmes

- provide training in empathy, communication and assertiveness skills, social skills, crisis-intervention strategies, understanding violence and human rights

- demonstrate to students, staff and parents how to follow school procedures and intervene when they witness bullying, and

- make sure that the whole school takes the anti-bullying message seriously.

External consultants:

- need to be bullying experts from the fields of psychology and social work, educational organisations, university departments and child/adolescent guidance clinics, and

- provide the knowledge and skills that would take the average teacher or counsellor years to accumulate, simplify and incorporate effectively into their work.

Schools can create a broader perspective by inviting other specialists, e.g. lawyers, police, human rights speakers and drama groups – parents, staff and students pay more attention to experts who are explicit, confronting, and deliver a strong message using their professional presentation skills.

SOME TRAINING PARTICULARS
1. For students

- All students need to understand what bullying involves, their school's role, the target's and the bully's perspective, and their role as the peer group.

- All students benefit from learning how to support, show empathy, intervene and resolve conflicts.

- The majority of bullying incidents are witnessed by peers. When they intervene, they are successful 50 percent of the time.

- Students should show their displeasure and discomfort with bullying and disassociate themselves from it.

- They need to report the bullying without fear of being labelled, e.g. 'dobber', 'rat', 'tattletale', 'whistleblower', etc.

- When older students befriend or mentor younger ones – via buddy programmes, peer support groups, sibling support or peer counselling support – they can reduce or prevent bullying.

- Skills for students include self-esteem building, mediation, negotiation and conflict resolution skills, motivation, cooperative learning and problem-solving skills, stress management and anger resolution skills, empathy, assertiveness training and social skills.

- There are many learning styles e.g. poster or retort competitions, role play, educational dramas (conflict resolution, video recording, puppets, videos, films, audio visual interactive programmes, debates), board games, books, websites, martial-arts programmes.

2. For school staff

All staff, from the principal down, need to relay the anti-bullying message. They need to build a cohesive, responsible, safe school culture to provide a framework for programmes and policies so students can report without fear. Kids notice everything: staff need to be role models of respect and empathy, and not bully themselves. To do this, they need to explore any relevant issues from their past around bullying (at school or elsewhere).

They require training to understand, provide support and incorporate anti-bullying practices into the class, curriculum or other areas such as the school bus, camp, library, canteen and playground. They need procedures to help all children, such as obtaining the different perspectives of the bullying game, maintaining records, reporting any wrongdoing, and following all school guidelines. They require basic assertive communication and counselling skills to assist the target and confront the bully.

Staff need to:

- create a positive social climate and provide students with a sense of belonging, e.g. reward random acts of kindness, give prizes for respectful behaviours (such as in sport)

- foster activities which develop empathy, e.g. class discussion, circle time, circle of friends (for students at risk), focus groups, meetings, role-plays, games, worksheets and cooperative learning strategies

- develop classroom protocols, strategies, structures, rules, slogans and consistent reinforcement to reduce bullying, e.g. 'No put-downs', 'Be a mate – support your peers', 'DOB – don't obey bullies', 'Bullying is banned', 'Back off'

- empower onlookers and peers to intervene appropriately

- structure the classroom so that bullies are under surveillance and targets are protected

- not ignore or say 'Do nothing or walk away', but protect vulnerable children and teach them how to protect themselves in future

- support children with limited social skills to join in school activities

- coach bullies and provocative students to relate with respect so that their behaviours don't boomerang back on them

- assist angry or scared parents while remaining firm, calm, empathic, neutral and respecting confidentiality

- refer the student for counselling within the school or externally if there is no improvement after three or four weeks, and

- discuss with the principal and parents if the child needs a new start at another school.

3. For parents

Bullying is a family concern. Schools that work systematically with parents will be more successful. Schools need to understand that although parents know their children better, they have their blind spots. They don't realise what their child is doing to be a target or bully, they can't acknowledge their child's limited social skills or emotional resources. They may deny their responsibility in assisting their children to alter their behaviours and acquire better social skills. Schools need to understand that parents can remain extremely angry long after their child stops being targeted and has made good friends. Parents and their children require validation. Schools need to educate parents of bullies that intervention can provide their child with the rights and skills to enjoy a normal life.

Schools need to:

- involve parents in the formulation of relevant policies and preventative programmes

- educate parents about bullying in all its forms, friendship skills, effective parenting and resilience-building in their children

- offer written material – books, handouts, contracts, seminars, newsletters, emails – and support and training, e.g. mobile phone/chat rules

- inform parents about bullying intervention procedures and protocols, including designated staff, maintaining contact and feedback (in person, by email, letter or phone), rules and consequences, and a timeframe for resolving difficulties

- organise parent–teacher meetings and make them more attractive via giveaways (e.g. chocolates or raffles) and services such as childcare or transport assistance; and maybe make them compulsory for unmotivated parents

- collaborate with parents who may otherwise sabotage the school's role and their children's needs

- involve parents at school via parent committees, playground supervision, mentoring, student presentations, joint projects and sports coaching, and

- refer children for internal or external assistance and, if all else fails, refer the child to another school.

7. Improve the physical environment

The school needs to identify the 'hot spots' where bullying occurs and re-design them, provide extra supervision, install surveillance cameras/metal detectors or employ guards. Although school facilities vary, any attempt to improve the school environment – such as wider laneways, student posters in corridors, attractive gardens, extra seating, a friendly classroom design, making it generally more attractive and welcoming – will help students feel valued.

- Use peer support, senior students, parents or teachers on yard duty to increase supervision and student safety. Bright vests or caps increase their visibility for small children.

- Provide safe havens for vulnerable students, e.g. a shady area near the staffroom.

- Provide extra sporting or other noncompetitive activities at lunchtimes: students will have better social experiences, be less bored and less likely to bully.

- Change classroom cliques and separate bully gangs by constructive involvement in school activities.

- Turn off library computers and create games for shy, sensitive students, or encourage them to participate in yard activities rather than remain isolated in the computer room/library the whole week.

- Create the means for frightened children to anonymously report the bullying, e.g. a school telephone, email address or sealed report box.

8. Implement crisis management

Schools need a structure to intervene immediately if bullying is taking place – and intervene as soon as possible, like the referee during a football game, instead of hoping it will resolve itself. This reinforces the school's policy that bullying will not be condoned and that constructive action will follow. Students can then trust the school to support them and can report without fear. As one counsellor said, 'It's important for kids to know that they will be heard and supported, so if you go to Mr Fisher, it stops.'

- Schools need a variety of intervention methods at their disposal, to select what is appropriate at the time to deal with the bullying.

- There are at least two parties to the bullying game, and everyone needs to know that they will be given a fair go.

- Children sabotage if threatened. The goal is respectful resolution, not blaming and shaming.

- Beware of interventions that wrongly empower or disempower. This can happen in mediation if a teacher forces a terrified target to confront the bully or bullies and resolve their conflict without empowering the target with assertive communication skills or providing consequences for the non-empathic bullies. The bully can thus overpower the target once again.

- Non-punitive or restorative practices should replace punitive or retributive ones where possible.

- Confidentiality must be maintained.

- Beware of parents who seek revenge! This role model is unacceptable.

- Clearly, it is inappropriate to gather a huge cast when a simple chat between two 'friends' may suffice, or when an external referral is warranted.

- Training programmes will reduce bullying incidents as children develop mediation skills to resolve incidents themselves.

Methods for managing bullying incidents

Schools can be very busy, stressful places. Any teacher can be confronted at any time by a target in the middle of the corridor or in the playground. They need to identify an appropriate method to use at the time.

The simple approach

The teacher or student approaches the target or bully and finds out what is going on, e.g. 'I've heard that Julie has been saying mean things about you. How do you feel about that?', 'You have changed lately. What's wrong?', 'Why have you been away so much?', 'I've just seen you do/say something that's against our school rules. If you don't stop, you know the consequences.'

In most cases a warning should suffice. However, if the bullying continues, follow school policy. Schools may require a combined approach of peer mediation, conflict resolution and/or sanctions depending on the whole story.

Peer mediation

This involves older students being trained to intervene in the schoolyard or elsewhere. They can be easily identified by a cap or a vest. This method is useful when targets have the confidence to report and the mediator has the school to support them in following up difficult incidents.

The method of shared concern

This problem-solving approach is designed to encourage students to co-exist and take responsibility for their own behaviours rather than identify targets and perpetrators. The mediator gathers information from staff first, then meets each student individually and encourages each bully to show concern for their target. The bully is then asked for constructive suggestions about how *she* can help the target. This is followed by a meeting with the target to explore her role in the bullying game. Finally, the mediator conducts a meeting with the class or the year concerned to build their social conscience and maintain improvements.

The no-blame approach

The teacher or counsellor acts as a mediator, interviewing the target first, then meeting the bully, her group, and others who could exert a positive influence, to relay the target's distress. They usually meet without the target. The students are not blamed, but are encouraged to become supportive and demonstrate responsibility for helping the target. The teacher follows up with the target and the group after a few weeks.

Restorative practices

This method is democratic, respectful and empathic. All parties involved are brought together, in small or larger groups, including targets, bullies, onlookers, staff and parents. A trained facilitator using a precise procedure conducts the session. Each person gives her side of the story and describes the impact on her. Then the facilitator structures the session to help participants resolve differences, repair harm and restore relationships. The focus is on developing empathy, dealing with conflict, teaching responsibility, making amends and negotiating solutions. The school system is also investigated and made accountable. An agreement or contract is made, and its progress is reviewed later on.

As this procedure can be difficult and time-consuming to implement, schools can also use a restoration philosophy, creating a structure whereby the target and the bully both express their feelings, and are then required to resolve their differences and create a fair resolution.

Legal action

Unfortunately, in a litigious society some parents sue and schools retaliate. It is a winning game for lawyers; everyone else loses, especially the child. Ideally, schools should resort to restorative practices or mediation to resolve a legal dispute respectfully. Most schools can't offer bully-free environments and comprehensive anti-bullying programmes, but nevertheless they *must* follow their own policies. If expert opinion is required, it can't be based only on the school's limitations in this area, as reflected by its policies and programmes, but also on whether or not it treated the child and her family reasonably and fairly in the circumstances.

9. Have consequences for breaking the rules

Schools need to specify the rules of conduct and provide a fixed and escalating series of consequences for students who interfere with designated behaviour boundaries and disobey the anti-bullying policy. To illustrate the importance of this, one of the perpetrators of the massacre at Columbine High, Colorado was a bully who was never charged over a date rape allegation; nor was he ever booked for parking his car in the wrong spot every day.

- Don't drive bullies underground. Sanctions need to reflect inappropriate behaviours expressed in politically correct terms, e.g. 'uncaring behaviours', 'forgetting social manners', 'phone misuse'.

- Warn the offender several times, suggest better strategies, use deterrents (such as push-ups, cleaning toilets), refer to a social skills or an anger management programme, exclude from a school function.

- Consequences could become cumulative throughout the school, excluding offenders from future significant school social events, sporting programmes, etc.

- After two or three warnings, involve senior staff, parents and refer for individual and family therapy.

- Further offences require discipline, e.g. detentions, a public apology, suspension. Schools may need to expel bullies who don't improve with family therapy.

The following example is to encourage schools to share their successes and to find new methods. Don't just adopt the latest trend. Teachers working at the ground level can be very creative and innovative as they find simple ideas that work with their children. For instance, Paul McBride has been developing a small, simple incident and observation booklet that teachers can use in the yard and maintain as part of the school records.

A success story

Some time ago, Karen McDonald, a primary-school counsellor, sent me a copy of her policies and programmes. The rules are firm, fair and final, and the amount of bullying at her school has seriously decreased. Each year students watch a video about the anti-harassment rules. They discover that offences for bullying are cumulative throughout their school days, and that these offences can seriously affect their participation in future sporting and other major social events.

When a child feels offended, she can report the incident, which leads to either a documented offence or a 'confront'. The child has a choice: she can simply report it, which means the bully receives a long-term punishment; or she can ask for a 'confront' with the bully in Karen's office, which leads to a scripted meeting between the target, the bully and Karen. This provides the bully with an opportunity to avoid trouble (i.e. a documented offence, or 'write-up') and makes school comfortable for the target, and also turns the tables so the bully has to watch her step to avoid a write-up and the accompanying consequences. Karen says, 'I empower the target to speak to the bully to tell her how she feels and ask her to stop. Then I say, "You are very lucky: X decided not to report you. You need to thank X, promise her it will never happen again, and promise that this meeting is confidential. If one of your friends finds out, I'll report you myself." I make the target swear to report the bully if she breaks her word. The bully thanks the target, makes her promises, and they shake hands. I tell the target that I will review the situation to make sure the bully is keeping her word. This forces the bully to blame herself for any offences, and it works.'

10. Offer individual assistance within the school

Students and parents need access to trained, professional school-based staff, and students need to know who they are and where they can be found. Schools need to help the target and her family deal with the painful impact of the bullying, take responsibility for her behaviours, and help her learn social survival skills. They need to respectfully assist bullies to handle the accusations and to develop empathy, and their families to develop appropriate parenting patterns. Remember that vulnerable children who feel embarrassed and upset will not go to just anyone.

- The school counsellor/guidance officer/educational psychologist/ social worker is ideal, especially if he or she covers a variety of areas – then children won't fear stigma and labelling, because they could be seeing him or her for another issue, e.g. study methods, career choice.

- Many schools have designated, trained, support staff, e.g. student welfare coordinators, pastoral care teacher, school nurse, chaplain, year level coordinator.

- Schools without access to a resident counsellor require consultant mental health professionals with the time, resources and expertise to deal with school bullying.

- Bullies know which behaviours are acceptable or not. If they experience a downward spiral in the future, they may sue the school for not providing them with adequate help earlier on.

11. Refer for external treatment

Schools cannot be expected to counsel severely depressed, distressed, difficult or disturbed children and dysfunctional families. Such cases need to be referred after a few months to psychologists, psychiatrists or other mental health professionals. Unfortunately, stigma, professional fees, denial, pride and false hope stop many parents seeking professional help. However, for parents who outlay hundreds of dollars on electronic 'blah blah' and holidays, the price is negligible compared to having a happy, socially confident kid. Besides, bullying can cause severe anxiety disorders and depression. Parents need to regard it as a medical danger, and respond accordingly when their child is affected. Ideally, schools should insist upon referral for external counselling when necessary and fund these sessions where possible, or find alternative sources of funding for parents on limited incomes, e.g. crimes compensation, child guidance clinics.

- Dealing with bullying doesn't take long: bullies and targets require an average of four to eight sessions with an experienced psychologist.

- The goal is to involve both parents in the first session to obtain the whole story, de-sensitise, re-frame, reprogramme faulty beliefs, assess the injury, validate and begin empowering the family.

- Subsequent sessions build confidence, provide options and teach bully-blocking skills.

- It could involve role-play, video-camera work, homework and feedback to parents to prevent potential sabotage.

- Once the student feels safe and is no longer bullied or bullying, she can learn social survival skills to develop a good bunch of friends and build a support network.

Therapy should produce physical, psychological, academic and social improvements. Look for two levels of change:

1. First order change – the child is able to deal with bullying and make a good bunch of true friends.

2. Second order change – she is happier at home (as relatives and parents observe), her schoolwork improves, and she has fewer health difficulties.

12. Evaluate

Although the total elimination of bullying remains a distant goal, it is important to review the culture and find out if targets are coping, bullies are behaving, and if the peer group feels empowered and safe. Schools need to monitor their policies, programmes and interventions each year to make sure that they are reducing bullying. They should obtain objective measures to confirm their effectiveness, e.g. improved academic results, fewer discipline issues. Then they can modify, discard and update where appropriate.

Key points

- Schools must respect their ethical and legal obligations to provide a safe learning environment.
- The school community includes students, teachers, parents, the school board, the local community, etc.
- Schools have many options to reduce bullying.

What to do

- Investigate: what is the school doing at present? Does it promote emotional and social resilience? What options does it have?

PART THREE

THE SIX SECRETS OF RELATING

Children and adults cope better with life stressors when they belong to a caring support network. Thus, human beings need to be social beings. Resilience depends on your social survival skills – how you relate to yourself and others. This is the basis of 'The Six Secrets of Relating'. It is a synthesis of my personal and professional life.

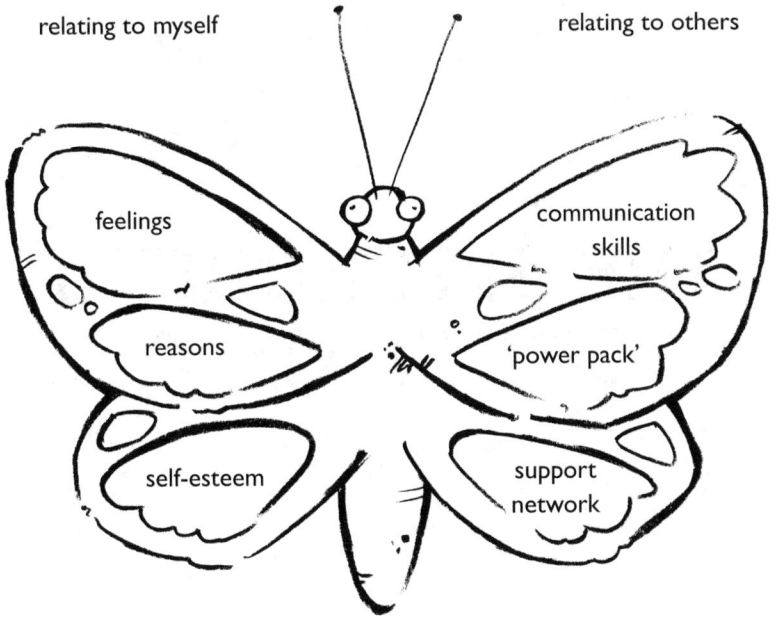

The butterfly symbolises growth and metamorphosis – the key to developing into a social being. These 'Six Secrets of Relating' form a generic, circular model useful in any context to develop emotional and social resilience in children, adolescents and adults. The first three secrets relate to your inner world; the second three to the outer world.

Use this model as you need it, rather than strictly adhering to the sequence in which it appears.

The Six Secrets involve learning new skills, so Part Three is directed at your child, although it will help you, too. (The few sections for parents in Part Three are tagged with either a 'Parents activity' icon or a 'Parents and kids activity' icon.) I want the children reading this to feel as though I am speaking to them directly, as I would in my office, to help them make appropriate changes in their behaviours. If your child is too young to read, spend ten minutes at night reading The Six Secrets together and discussing them. Even young children will understand the concepts.

Note: As this part of the book is addressed mainly to your child, 'you' usually means him or her.

8

Regulate your feelings –
Secret 1

Sean had been teased and excluded since beginning high school. They picked on him because he was Asian, although he'd lived most of his life in America. At first he was stunned – he didn't know what to do. Everything he tried, including asking the school for help, had failed. As time wore on he became angry, then scared. Finally he gave up – he felt powerless and paralysed.

Bullying arouses many bad feelings like fear, anger, shame, hurt, confusion and powerlessness because it interferes with so many aspects of your life. It seems that girls get sad and boys get mad. You either implode or explode. It's uncomfortable being bullied, witnessing it, or being a bully. Earlier on, I described the 'fight or flight' instinct. This survival instinct is your internal safety sensor. Your brain identifies a threat to your safety, then it sends a message to your adrenal glands re-questing energy to take action. A cocktail of biochemical survival hormones are released to enable you to fight or flee. These hormones influence everything you do, from eating and running to feeling, thinking and behaving. Like many other things, too much is not always best. You can't handle bullying while your body is crammed and jammed with excessive amounts of stress-related hormones such as adrenaline, noradrenaline, cortisol, norepinephrine and epinephrine. Unless you regulate and release your feelings, you'll become powerless, paralysed or 'bottle and burst', hurting yourself or someone else in the process. Regardless of whether you ignore the consequences or exacerbate the situation by challenging the bully, you become more vulnerable.

But once you regulate your painful feelings, especially anger and fear, you can think more clearly and develop a sensible plan to block the bully. You'll appear more relaxed and less likely to make the bully happy. Other children will support you because you are 'cool'. Thus, dealing with feelings gets you into action.

Bullies have feelings too!

Apart from the small minority of bullies who enjoy bullying, most ordinary bullies don't mean to hurt. There may be numerous reasons why they bully, such as being rebuffed, threatened or controlled by the group. However, their internal security wiring system is the same as everyone else's: most bullies are just trying to survive in the best way they know.

Bullies sense your fear and attack first to protect themselves from being attacked (see Chapter 5). They fight first because they have learnt that from past experiences. Alternatively, bullies sense your anger or fear, and this reminds them of their own painful feelings inside, so they attack you to expel their pain. When an ordinary bully can't detect your fear or anger, they lose power and stop. That's why I say, 'If you show fear or anger, you make a bully happy.'

How some kids feel about bullying

Natalie: 'When I am teased I feel hurt inside.'

Shane: 'If someone hits me, I feel so angry that I want to hit back.'

Jane: 'When someone teases me for no reason, I feel confused and don't know what to do.'

Ben: 'I didn't care at first and ignored it. Then I couldn't wait for the end of the year. I hate this school and I want to leave.'

Rob: 'I can't be bothered doing my homework. Nobody plays with me.'

Maria: 'She is so sensitive, so I like teasing her.'

The major feelings

Human beings can experience many different emotions, but they can be simplified into four basic feelings: happiness, sadness, anger and fear (or 'glad, sad, mad and bad'). Just like the prime colours of red, blue and yellow – which create a variety of shades of colour – there are numerous varieties and combinations of feelings (see later in this chapter).

The major feelings

glad	sad
happy, ecstatic, elated, blissful, excited, elated, pleased, jovial, peaceful, cheerful, joyful, jolly, good, contented, satisfied	depressed, gloomy, sombre, dismal, feeling blue, sorrowful, dejected, glum, miserable, woeful, unhappy, melancholy
mad	**bad**
angry, fuming, livid, annoyed, furious, ruffled, frustrated, irritated, exasperated, frenzied, provoked, cross, irate, enraged, incensed	anxious, scared, fearful, uptight, apprehensive, confused, uneasy, stressed, nervous, panicky, worried, concerned, edgy, tense, terrified, pressured, restless, frightened

How do you feel about being bullied?

Kids activity

Write down the words that apply to you (e.g. frustrated, afraid, painful, upset, sick, worried, resentful, bad, terrible, revengeful, horrible, hatred, embarrassed, painful, powerless, helpless, stuck, stupid, silly, fed up, down, discouraged, weak, miserable, poor self-esteem, vulnerable, lose confidence, worthless, hurt, upset, small, unwelcome, unwanted, no friends, isolated, I don't belong, left out, lonely).

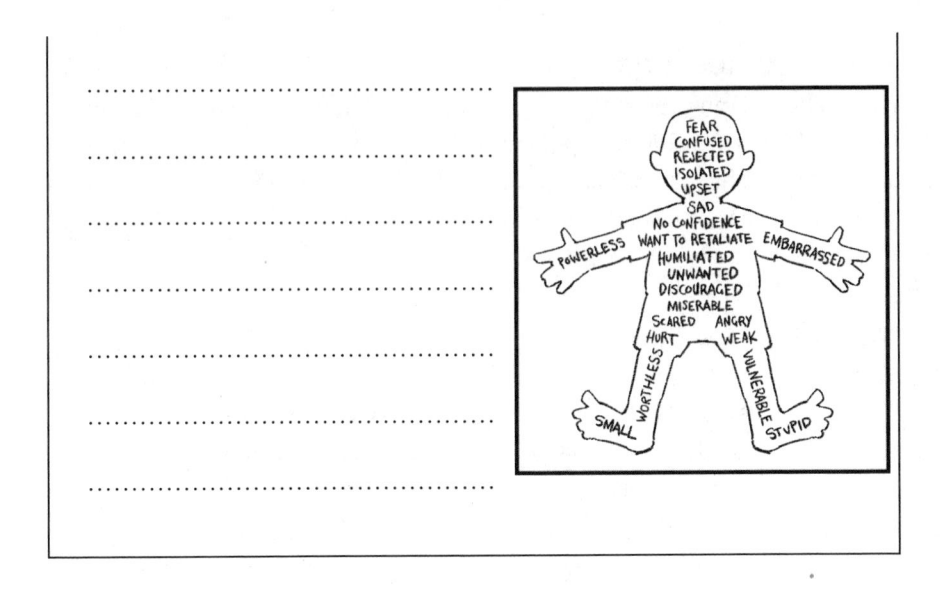

Do you lose, abuse or use your power?

You can express your feelings in three different ways: passive, aggressive or assertive. Passive children lose their power, aggressive children abuse their power, while assertive children use their power. Most children can lose, abuse or use their power at different times.

1. Passive or passive-aggressive

When you express your feelings passively, you are emotionally constipated. No-one at home or school knows the true story. You pretend and say, 'I'm okay, I'm not upset, everything's alright'. Perhaps you expect others to guess what you are feeling, but they underestimate it. Sadly, most teachers and kids can't be bothered understanding a child who bottles up her feelings.

Despite what you say, your actions show your pain and discomfort, so you might clench your hand and look as though you are about to cry. You look miserable and depressed, stuff yourself with chocolate or hide in a book or a computer. You become more isolated, misunderstood and unsupported.

You become passive-aggressive when you spread nasty gossip, exclude or complain about someone behind their back instead of to their face, or when you show your pain to your parents but say, 'I don't want to talk about it'. They know something is wrong but they can't help you, so they feel bad. Then you release your anger by having a tantrum or being mean at home – using the 'bottle and burst' method. *Passive children lose their power because they can't help themselves.*

2. Aggressive

When you are being aggressive, you make a grand display of your feelings, e.g. make a big fuss over studying for a test, when you've hurt your finger or when you've done well at school. You vomit your angry feelings all over others – you yell at other kids, shout at your family, break and throw things, physically hurt, kick and punch others. You might be upset, but you don't realise the toxic impact of your emotions as they explode over other people. Whether you're a target or bully, you can be aggressive at home and provocative at school, making things worse. When you're aggressive, others will become angry or scared. They will back away or retaliate. *Aggressive children abuse their power and make the situation worse.*

3. Assertive

You are being assertive when you identify your feelings, such as feeling safe, comfortable or threatened. You check if you are feeling happy, sad, angry or scared. Then you work out when and how to release these feelings. You listen to your gut feelings to protect yourself, then show signs of friendliness, use direct 'I' statements when suitable (see Chapter 11), ask for help or release your bad feelings in constructive ways, e.g. sport. You use self-respect to protect yourself, without being disrespectful or destructive to others. You use assertiveness skills like an emotional sunscreen. *Assertive children use their power effectively to create a win-win situation.*

Here are some examples of each type of behaviour.

Passive, aggressive or assertive?

Bully	Child replies or behaviour	Evelyn's comments
Bully says, 'You're fat.'	**Passive:** 'I'm not fat.'	'You look and sound upset.'
	Aggressive: 'And you're stupid.'	'Your anger shows the bully that the truth upsets you.'
	Assertive: 'No, I'm nicely padded.'	'The bully is stuck when you are cool, calm and confident.'

Bully excludes: 'You can't play with us today.'	**Passive:** 'Why can't I play with you?' **Aggressive:** 'I'm going to tell the teacher.' **Assertive:** 'Thanks for telling me.'	'Nobody wants to play with an unhappy child.' 'The teacher can't do anything, those kids are mean, while you are threatening.' 'You find nicer kids to play with.'
Bully punches and kicks: 'Go away.'	**Passive:** Upset, cries, slinks off. **Aggressive:** Retaliates, punches and kicks back. **Assertive:** Tickles her under her armpits.	'This child behaves like a loser.' 'This child gives her power to the bully and the fight begins.' 'This child blocks the bully's game or says, "This is a warning: do that again and I'll report you."'

Parents activity

Lose, abuse or use?

How does your child behave? Note the behaviours that describe your child, use feedback from others.

Loser statements:	'I don't care', 'I'm alright', 'I don't mind'.
Loser behaviours:	Complain, do nothing, 'bottle and burst', eyes and head down, pay back quietly, hunched over, quiet, mumbling voice, pale, looks miserable, teary, doesn't smile often.
Abusive statements:	'You're an idiot', 'Don't touch me', 'You're just as bad', 'Why don't you shut up?'

Abusive behaviours:	Angry face, loud voice, nasty look, blame, complain, sarcastic, mean, retaliate, provoke, attack back, threatening stance, rigid, tense, throw or break things.
Useful statements:	'I don't like you doing that', 'I'm angry at you', 'I need help', 'I don't think you're being fair', 'I don't like being your friend any more'.
Useful behaviours:	Stand up straight, confident body language, be calm and pleasant, firm eye contact, clear voice, neutral-looking face, choose appropriate words.

Bully behaviours

Do you have empathy for your target or not? Adults and kids expect feedback when they tell you how they feel – 'I feel…when you…'.

If you feel bad about hurting her feelings, you can say:

'I'm sorry.'

'I didn't realise.'

'I didn't mean to hurt.'

'Come and play.'

You can change from bullying to behaving.

The feelings formula

1. Identify: What do you feel?

2. Quantify: How much? Is it comfortable or uncomfortable?

3. Release: How to release these feelings?

1. Identify: What do you feel?

The first step in blocking bullying is to identify the painful feelings you have about the bullying game. You need to check out your anger, fear and sadness (you won't be happy until you are smiling naturally). You can use the feedback from others to make sure you have identified all your feelings and behaviours. Look for these painful feelings all over your body: they could be hiding anywhere, inside or out. They are your survival instinct, warning you to confront or leave the bullying game. These feelings empower you to protect yourself and get help. You will go on to release the painful feelings, share your story with those you trust, work out your options, block the bullying and improve your friendships.

THE BODY CHART
Use the above chart to pinpoint your feelings whenever you feel uncomfortable, e.g. you may feel fear in your stomach and anger in your hands. If you draw a larger chart, you can colour in all your feelings, including painful and happy ones. You can use any colours you like, or else red = mad, orange = bad, blue = sad, and yellow = glad. You can also use a combination of colours to represent a mixture of feelings, e.g. shame = anger + sadness (red and blue), embarrassment = anger + fear + sadness (red, orange and blue), and so on.

2. Quantify: How much? Is it comfortable or uncomfortable?

Once you identify your feelings, you then need to calculate – using a score out of ten – how much they are affecting you. If the score is above four or five out of ten, they will be uncomfortable. Younger children can quantify their feelings by saying, 'Little', 'Medium' or 'Lots'. Then you can take the appropriate steps to release them.

Kids activity

Write down some of your feelings:

I am really glad that..

I feel sad that...

I am really feeling scared about...

I am angry that...

BULLYMETER

3. Release: How to release these feelings?

Now you need to work out how to release your feelings appropriately. There are three main ways to release feelings: biochemical (direct or indirect), verbal (direct or indirect), and physical (direct or indirect) release. Remember, it doesn't matter what you use, as long as it works!

BIOCHEMICAL RELEASE

You should not consider pharmaceutical drugs of any kind unless it's an emergency.

Direct: Bach Rescue Remedy, St John's Wort (check with your doctor);

Indirect: Comfort food, dark chocolate (70+ percent), aromatherapy, chamomile tea.

VERBAL RELEASE (SEE ALSO CHAPTER 9)

The simplest way to release your emotional pain is to inform the bully how you feel about the bullying. If this is unsafe, then inform someone else about the bullying to get support. Either way, you obtain immediate feedback. This shows you whether they care or not about your feelings, and it shows that you take responsibility for your feelings, and leaves the door open to resolution. It gives a clear message without blaming and shaming. This is very easy for some people but difficult for others, and may depend on your family and culture. You need to practise the 'I' word with an adult.

Direct: To bully: 'I'm upset when you make fun of my family.'

'I'm angry that you take my rulers and pencils.'

To a student: 'I'm sad that you can't tell the bully to stop.'

'I'm happy you include me in your group.'

Indirect: To your parent: 'I'm angry about the mean kid who teases me.'

'I'm frightened that I'll be laughed at in front of those kids.'

To your teacher/counsellor: 'I'd like you to stop those kids bullying me.'
'Please speak to   a bout not pushing me in the yard.'

Safety instructions

Be aware that some kids don't mean to hurt, while others do want to hurt you. If you confront nasty bullies – e.g. 'I don't like you being mean to me' or 'I'm very angry at you for spreading rumours behind my back' – they will be happy. They want you to be upset, then they can bully you again, laugh in your face or say mean things like, 'Piss off'. So only confront unkind bullies who aren't always mean.

Bonus verbal tricks

Kids activity

- Find somewhere safe to yell: your bedroom, the car, into a cushion, in the shower.

- Sound out the words you feel very slowly, emphasising and stressing each letter at a time, e.g. SCARED, say: SSS…CCC…AAA…RRR…EEE…DDD. Try words such as: ANGRY, SHOCKED, MISERABLE, DEPRESSED, FURIOUS, EMBARRASSED. This is a simple way to release feelings.

- Swear in other languages and create nonsense swear words – you can't get into trouble if no-one understands you.

PHYSICAL RELEASE

Many children don't like talking about their feelings, especially boys. However, the biochemical hormones causing your pain need to be released even though it's difficult, otherwise the bully (and his gang) knows you are vulnerable. If you were feeling bad and went for a very long walk, a bike ride or climbed the stairs of a 50-storey building, you might feel physically tired, but you'd be less angry, tense or upset than before. Perhaps you've seen a really funny movie and laughed until your sides hurt – any painful feelings you had beforehand would have vanished.

When you do something physical, you breathe in a lot of oxygen. This sets up a biochemical chain reaction in your body and neutralises your painful feelings.

It's impossible to feel as bad as you did before. Your caveman ancestors released feelings through physical activity all the time. So did kids before electronic 'blah blah' was invented. There are many simple activities or exercises that release painful feelings. Anything is good as long as it works. Adults need to encourage and supervise you.

Direct: Hit a cushion, kick a ball, throw darts, lift weights.

Indirect: Do a visualisation exercise, play basketball, stack wood, wash the car.

SOME TIPS ON RELEASING FEELINGS

- *Check your comfort score*: Everyone knows what it's like to feel hungry, thirsty or needing the toilet. If you're feeling peckish, you might snack, but if you're very hungry you need a real meal. If you're in the mood for something sweet, one chocolate might do, but if you're feeling blue, you might binge on a whole packet of biscuits. Some people snack every few hours while others only eat at meal times. Thus, if you are a little sad or annoyed, e.g. 3/10, it won't affect your behaviour very much. But if you are feeling a 4/10 or more, it affects your behaviour and makes a bully happy. You need to release these painful feelings as soon as possible to feel comfortable inside. Then you can take action to block a bully and enjoy life.

- *How often?* Plan how often you need to release your pain. If you're not very sad, bad or mad, you can release it three times a day, such as at morning, lunchtime and after school. If your pain is above 7/10 every day, then release it five times a day. If your score is very high, e.g. 9/10, release every two hours to prevent emotional build-up. Once you feel safe or less discomfort, e.g. 3/10, you can just release at the weekend.

- *Quick fixes*: You'll need some quick techniques for feeling better during the school day, e.g. take ten deep breaths, do a brief visualisation (of happy holiday times, for instance) or cuddle your teddy bear. These techniques have to work in class, in the school grounds and on your way to and from school.

- *Collect a variety*: You need a variety of techniques to use, depending on your mood and what's happening at the time. Some are useful everywhere, including school, while others take time and are more suitable at home and on weekends, e.g. a bike ride, reading, hobbies. You can invent your own techniques and ask other people for suggestions. In this book there are lots of ideas – choose what feels right for you. Although some appear basic and simple, they work for very traumatised people and may help you.

Release your anger

- Exercise, walk, jog, run, swim, skip, hit, throw, stretch, do push-ups, punch, kick.

- Blow up balloons, play with marbles, tear up newspaper.

- Write in a journal.

- Write bad things down and burn the paper in a safe place (with parental help).

- Use a punching bag (fill with sand, or stuff a hessian bag with wet newspaper and let it dry).

- Squeeze hard plasticine, clay or stuffed toys, crack walnuts open with your hands.

- Throw chunks of ice or corks; throw a wrapped bar of chocolate and then eat the pieces.

- Go somewhere quiet and cool down.

- Listen to loud music, play a musical instrument loudly, sing or whistle.

- Do some energetic dancing, e.g. Spanish, Irish or tap dancing.

- Get a plain calico doll that you can throw, draw on, stamp on, stab, burn – just pretend it's the bully!

- Learn martial arts, e.g. karate, Tai Kwon Do or judo.

- Add your own favourite techniques…

Deal with your stress and anxiety

- Do instant deep breathing.

- Relax physically and mentally with yoga or Tai Chi.

- Give and receive a massage (if alone, massage your feet and hands).

- Have a bubble bath or use essential oils.

- Hold crystals, a stress ball, a teddy bear, jewellery, prayer beads.

- Blow bubbles.

- Remember times when you felt really happy.

- Go shopping: buy a little treat, e.g. a small bag of mixed sweets.

- Exercise: gym, aerobics, run up and down lots of stairs.

- Find a new hobby – knitting or doing a jigsaw releases tension.

- Do some pet therapy: play with a pet, keep goldfish.

- Be with friends: have fun, read joke books, cartoons, watch funny videos, play games.

- Delegate your worries: use worry dolls at night.

- Visualise, e.g. journey in your mind to a special calming place.

- Add your own favourite techniques…

Deal with your sadness

- Release tears: peel an onion, eat hot chilli peppers or horseradish.

- Listen to sad music, watch a sad movie, read/write sad poems.

- Do more pet therapy – watch birds, fish; visit the zoo or a pet shop.

- Meditate somewhere serene: a church, synagogue, mosque, cemetery.

- Do nature therapy: burn a candle or incense; watch a fire, a fountain, the sea.

- Do hug therapy: spend time with caring people.

- Go somewhere peaceful – near running water, a garden, the beach.

- Do an instinctive exercise: wrap your arms around yourself and rock slowly, backwards and forwards.

- Enjoy comfort food or drink (in moderation), e.g. chocolate, chicken soup, chips, tea.

- Add your own favourite techniques…

Feeling happy and positive

- Make a 'feelgood' list: enjoyable clothes, games, perfume, cuddly toy, good magazines, sweets, cubby house, hobbies, jewellery.

- Do something different, e.g. try different chocolate, change your hairstyle, redecorate your bedroom, go to school another way.

- Spend time doing enjoyable activities, e.g. sport, dancing, games, Internet chat.

- Find things that make you smile and laugh.

- Say or do something nice for someone else and check their reaction, e.g. smile at five people.

- Spend time with friends or family who are cheerful, fun and caring.

- If no-one is free, then phone someone from class you don't know very well and chat about schoolwork.

- Count up to five nice things people have said to you recently.

- Say nice things to yourself, e.g. 'I love me', 'I'm the best', or do something physically caring, e.g. give yourself a hug or a kiss.

- Fantasise about wonderful things happening to you very soon.

- Add your own favourite techniques…

Key points

- Bullying makes targets feel very bad, sad and mad.
- These negative feelings influence your behaviours.
- Release painful feelings to stop bullying.
- You can abuse, lose or use your power.

What to do

- You need to identify, quantify and release your feelings.
- Release feelings biochemically, verbally and physically.
- Develop a variety of techniques.
- Maintain a comfortable emotional state by releasing as often as appropriate.

9

Understand why you are bullied or a bully – Secret 2

Ben has three older brothers. There is a 10-year gap between him and his next brother – he was an unexpected but welcomed baby. His mother enjoyed being busy and needed. But Ben was often ill as a baby; his parents took him to the children's hospital at least five times. He is in high school now, and is healthy and strong, but his mother still fusses over him. His father is focused on his business: he doesn't have the time for him that he had for Ben's brothers when they were young. The older boys are busy with careers and girlfriends. Ben has become a real 'mummy's boy'. Of course, the kids at school know that he is different. They bully him and he fights back.

It's highly unlikely that you were born a target, a bully or both. Probably a variety of events happened over time that increased your likelihood of becoming involved in the bullying game. But this process can be reversed. You need to understand why it happened to you and not someone else. The echidna buries itself in the sand when attacked; similarly, many quiet, shy children are never bullied. Despite their limited social skills, they block or avoid bullying. Many height-, weight- and intellectually-challenged children aren't always bullied. Nor do all big children bully.

It is important to search for the reasons so that you don't waste your precious energy feeling humiliated, then blaming and shaming others – that only makes you powerless. Understanding the reasons will give you the courage to focus on what you can do to avoid the bullying game.

Below is a chart to help you find these reasons. Or, if you have been accused of being a bully, you can use the same mind map to work out where you didn't learn the appropriate empathy skills.

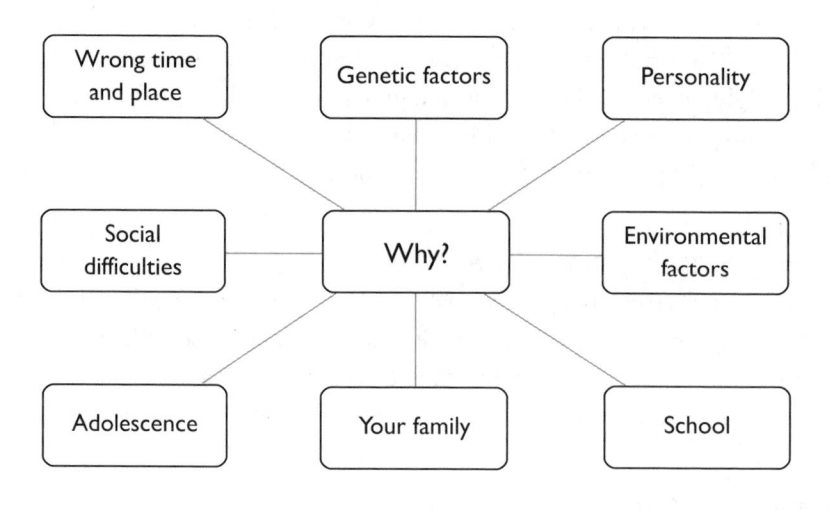

Wrong time and place

Sally was a bright, friendly, popular girl, then suddenly everything changed. The girls excluded her from everything, even over the holidays. She was dreadfully lonely. 'I can't understand what went wrong,' she told me. She mentioned that a very sick classmate had died before the bullying. It caused a huge shock. The school didn't provide opportunities for the girls to release their grief and guilt – they clung together for six weeks and then started attacking one another. Clearly, the girls found it easier to create 'bitchfights' than to deal with their unfinished grief. Sally was targeted. Unfortunately, she was in the wrong school at the wrong time.

There are numerous occasions when you could be in the wrong place at the wrong time. Not playing sport, having wealthy parents, or wearing glasses or braces means different things in different schools. If they are unacceptable at your school, you could encounter bullying.

Genetic factors

Nicole had difficulty reading; even the blackboard was hard to see. She had learning difficulties, her self-esteem was poor, and kids excluded her. Eventually one teacher became suspicious and suggested to her parents that she have an eye test. Once she was given glasses, her schoolwork improved and she learnt how to stop being bullied.

You can be targeted because you were born different. Being physically handicapped, clumsy, small or tall, having a different skin colour, unusual behaviours (e.g. a twitch or a stutter), scoliosis, eczema or epilepsy, crooked teeth, a big nose, bad eyesight, other health problems, and giftedness are some genetic factors that attract bullying. Or you could have been born more jealous or aggressive and have little empathy for vulnerable or indulged children.

Having learning difficulties

If you aren't as clever as your classmates or have learning difficulties, you may need specialised help. You may feel different or excluded socially. If you feel sensitive about your problems, you will interpret comments about them as insults and react aggressively or provocatively. You are then more likely to be targeted.

Being talented

If you are very bright and keen on schoolwork, then you could be targeted because you are different. However, you may make the situation worse without realising it. Serious kids often don't believe in chit-chat; they think it beneath them. Thus, you can alienate peers who may bully back. You might brag about how well you have done while denigrating students with schoolwork difficulties. They will retaliate. Or if you disguise your ability and pretend to be like everyone else, you lower your potential. The bully then senses your vulnerability and frustration at being different.

Personality

'Just because I'm new and try to do well in my work and don't get in trouble a lot, people tease me. They call me "goodie-goodie".
I ignore the teasing but it doesn't go away.'

If you were born more sensitive, you will have a lower tolerance to stress. Your sympathetic nervous system is more active than your peers'. You become upset and react. At home you are protected, but not at school. Your distress is clearly visible on your face, like the lights on a plane's instrument panel. You broadcast your vulnerability: your eyes look scared and teary, your lips quiver and your facial muscles twitch more rapidly, you blush or pale readily – revealing rapid changes in skin colour – and your anxiety is reflected in your voice, body language and words.

Alternatively, you may have been born an angrier child. Then you attack when things don't go your way, for example, if others don't follow your instructions. Perhaps you feel intimidated by clever or attractive kids and want to make them feel bad. Maybe you like to be in control so that you have a group to belong to. Alternatively, maybe you don't care about other people and can't feel empathy for them. They are there to be abused. You feel good when they feel bad.

The role of self-esteem

When you accept yourself just as you are, your self-esteem is healthy and it's easy to relate to others. You also respect your right to be safe. You insist on being protected by others or protecting yourself when others bully. Generally, children don't bother to bully secure, confident children. If your self-esteem is low, you feel bad about who you are and criticise yourself constantly. Your inner voice acts like a bully and makes you vulnerable. Bullies sense your secret. They look for your reaction, e.g. if you feel bad about your learning difficulties, the bully reads your feedback and bullies you about them. Or you may be blessed with wealthy parents and enjoy lovely holidays, and other children get jealous, e.g. 'So you've been to Disneyland…'. If you're extremely attractive, they might say, 'Hey ugly', and you may react with embarrassment. Remember, it's not your fault that you've been born lucky.

Bullying lowers your self-esteem, making it easier for others to hurt you or for you to react and retaliate. Then your self-esteem drops further if you are let down by others. If you bully, then your self-esteem will be good until your schoolwork deteriorates because you don't focus on your studies – and then you're forced to socialise with 'losers', because most kids want to socialise with kids who are achieving in later school years, not with dropouts.

Doing nothing

Many children handle bullying by doing nothing. Obviously, they are doing what adults told them to do. It seems like sound advice: if you do nothing, disguise your anger, fear or pain, you won't make a bully happy. But adults forget one major thing: kids aren't always good at following instructions. When they tell you to do nothing, you think you are but you are not! Instead, you look scared and act frustrated. You turn away or react, and bullies love you either way! Then, to make matters worse, you don't tell or remind adults that it is still happening.

Being provoked

You might be feeling highly stressed or angry. Let's face it, children can encounter many difficulties – e.g. personal tragedies such as a car accident, learning difficulties, sexual, emotional or physical abuse – and you may need to release your discomfort by jumping into a fight with the bully. If you are tense, hyperactive, frustrated or irritated, you make good bully fodder. Although it's useful to manipulate a bully to release your frustrations and blame someone else, it can boomerang back. The negative feedback reinforces your poor self-esteem, exacerbates the situation, and you are bullied again. Maybe you decide to ignore the bully, but once the pressure builds, you explode and fight back. This is when teachers who have seen nothing else blame you.

Social difficulties

Not everyone is sociable. Some children find it hard to be friendly and relate to a group of kids. You may have personal difficulties that affect your socialising. Perhaps you don't know how to begin a conversation, have fun or join in unorganised activities at lunchtime or recess. You may say or do the wrong thing, be very quiet and find social situations hard. Other children then see you as different.

If you are socially isolated, you advertise your vulnerability and are more likely to be bullied. You may react, irritate or aggravate to get attention. You may pretend to belong to a group even if its members bully you because you may prefer negative attention to none. Your reaction then leads to further bullying. Or perhaps you get attention by trying to control others instead of relating with respect and empathy.

An easy target feels ashamed and doesn't complain assertively. If your communication skills are poor, this handicaps you reporting and relating what happened in an assertive, objective manner to parents and teachers. Perhaps you are scared that you will blush, cry or embarrass yourself. Maybe you feel paralysed because your brain is releasing too many stress hormones. Unfortunately, your mates and schoolteachers can't understand or feel empathy for you, so you might be bullied further and feel even more powerless.

Shyness

Shy children find socialising with their peers difficult. You may have a few friends but not a group. You could be handcuffed to one friend to avoid loneliness. You are scared of being rejected so you avoid challenging anyone, even a friend. You are terrified of doing the wrong thing, and don't stand up for yourself when attacked. You react to stress by being very anxious or freezing up. You fear attention and embarrassment. You are left alone, unsupported by your peer group. If you're secretive, it's hard to tell your parents or teacher, so you become more isolated. Beware that making friends with a shy, aloof child is hard. When you reject children who are trying to be friendly, they will feel upset and may bully back.

Environmental factors

Bill was an extremely gifted musician but not sporty. Sadly, his peers valued sport, not music. They teased him mercilessly until he went to a school that respected musical talent.

Rebecca felt different at her old school so her parents sent her to a Jewish school, believing she would have more in common with the students there. But she found it hard to join in: she was quiet, and waited for others to invite her to play, whereas other students seemed more familiar with one another. They appeared to merge easily, like with family. So Rebecca had to learn a new set of social skills.

Children are affected by the attitudes of people around them. If you are different, these attitudes play a detrimental role. Most children have an obsession with being normal because 'being different' equals 'loser'. If your school favours academic results, you achieve; but if your school praises sporting prowess, you excel at sport. The definition of 'normal' varies from school to school. If you feel different from what is normal at your school, you remain invisible or react. In some schools you bully to retain your 'popular' status.

Being different

In schools and cultures that insist on a high level of conformity, children blame themselves for being different. A young Japanese girl told me about a cool, popular boy who had been teased once and then committed suicide, yet the boy who had teased him hadn't meant harm. In Japan everyone has to be the same with their clothes, behaviour, everything! But in America, everyone is encouraged to be different. Most children who are different to the peer group feel inferior. They might be homosexual, have an unusual name or dress differently. While most children laugh with their peers, you may be sensitive and react. The bully senses your self-denigration and attacks.

Relocation

Rod and his Australian parents have lived all over the world. He's been to a conservative school in Great Britain and an American-style school in the Middle East. He felt shy and intimidated by the extroverted American students in his class.

Millions of children are uprooted every year as families change residence or parents change jobs or are promoted, or because of financial reasons, marital separation or migration. They adapt as long as they can blend into the new culture. This includes adapting to new educational systems, local social systems and communication styles. For example, the verbal social skills of American children are usually superior to those of Australian children, who in turn are more eloquent than Asian students. Children generally find it easier to pick up new ways of socialising before they reach adolescence. Girls tend to find making new friendships easier than boys do: boys may not know how to blend in, and so are more likely to be rejected by peers. This is exacerbated when parents are relocated every few years.

Culture

> Betty's family came from Malaysia but live in Australia. She said, 'Good Chinese children show respect to their parents by hiding their feelings, especially their anger. It's called "being plain".'

When a child goes to a school where the prevailing culture is different from his own, he is expected to blend in and socialise e.g. a Muslim child attending a Christian school, or an Asian child attending an Anglo-Saxon school. Children who are proud of their religious or cultural heritage are seldom bullied. They respond assertively: 'I'm proud to be a Muslim' or, 'I like having a Jewish mother'. If you are ignorant or ashamed about your religion, culture or ethnic background – e.g. Indian, Chinese, Arabic, African, Koori, Jewish, Catholic, Maori or Muslim – you will feel bad about being different. If you show embarrassment about being different, you attract bullies. Understand that different cultures behave differently.

You may be oblivious to the values and customs of your new school. If you have an Asian background, your traditions may train you to be powerless in Western schools. If your culture demands safeguarding the family's name, i.e. 'saving face', then risking embarrassment seems a fate worse than death. Alternatively, if your culture expects you to fight back when family honour is threatened, you will become aggressive. And some other children may manipulate you to react in order to release their frustrations.

Adolescence

As children pass through puberty to adolescence, they face many developmental changes and challenges. Their body changes shape, their intelligence matures and their emotions fluctuate. They can be sweet one moment and spiteful the next. Bullying is at its worst during late primary and early secondary school, when most children are developing, changing and feeling very insecure. They rely on the group to reinforce their emerging personality.

Variation

Boys and girls grow and develop at different intellectual, social, cognitive and emotional rates. Children who develop earlier or later than their peer group feel sensitive about being different – for example, the girl whose period begins long before her peers' or who is not interested in boys when everybody else is, or the boy who is very small or tall in comparison to his peers. Bullies also feel vulnerable at this time and capitalise on their targets' sensitivity.

Sexuality

In addition to developing a physical, emotional, intellectual and social identity, you can be confused about your emerging sexual identity. Everyone experiences sensitivity about anything to do with sex, sexual activities and gender. Nobody wants to be called 'prostitute', 'gay', 'homo' or 'leso'. Everyone wants to be seen as being sexually normal, whatever that is. Some kids are too young to know, but they sense if something isn't 'right'. Most bullies reflect their own inner fears and confusion when they take advantage of a child's vulnerability to sexual taunts.

Two basic tasks

Every adolescent needs to develop a sense of how he scores as an individual ('Who am I?') and how he scores socially as compared to the peer group ('Do I belong?').

'WHO AM I?'

A typical example of a young person's dilemma is clothes: a child who refuses to wear what his mum buys ends up wearing the same as everyone else in his peer group. Once you accept, respect and understand yourself, you know who you are and you have an identity. When you feel good about who you are, you are less likely to be bullied. Then you find a bunch of true friends, and it doesn't matter what the peer group dictates. But many adolescents don't know who they are. If you feel vulnerable, you react to bullying.

If you are a target, you may relate to peers in some situations but not in others. You probably feel confident meeting a classmate at the airport or on holiday, where you are freer to socialise without risking peer-group disapproval. In fact, bullies are less likely to bully without their group, and even if they do, you feel less pain and shame. But you will feel more vulnerable the closer you get to school, as the bullying reflects your 'negative' status. However, you can change your identity like changing a mask: later on, you will worry less about 'popular' versus 'reject' groups and more about your career and social life. This is when the bully loses status – unless he bullies outside school, e.g. through relationships, work, local gangs or road rage.

'DO I BELONG?'

Adolescence is a critical time for developing social skills. Schools have three main groups:

1. The popular, cool, sporty or tough group represents social success.

2. The unpopular, nerds, quiet achievers and losers represent the reject group.

3. The average group occupies the middle. This group actually manipulates the popular and the unpopular groups to gauge their own social status. It promotes and demotes. Thus, the groups, gangs or cliques change constantly.

You spend your time mesmerised by your peer-group relationships and how you score socially. Boys tend to congregate in larger groups and de-value those who don't belong, e.g. the non-footballers. Girls prefer smaller groups and consolidate group membership by excluding those less socially acceptable. The peer group offers a pseudo or temporary identity; it establishes boundaries and is very powerful. Teenagers use their group like a passport photo – it represents their identity development. Many bullies belong to the social group until schoolwork handicaps their status, but some are quite unpopular.

Your family

As we saw in Chapter 3, family relationships influence your likelihood of becoming a target or a bully. If you are overvalued or undervalued at home, you are more likely to become a target or a bully. If your parents are overcontrolling or overprotective, they won't give you practice in handling disagreements. If your parents are inconsistent, allow changing boundaries or show abuse, you are more likely to bully.

Secrets

Donald was called 'egghead' and teased for years. The teachers and other kids saw him as tense and secretive. He was born premature with physical difficulties – his mother was scared he would die, and so overprotected him. At our last session, she casually mentioned that his twin had died at birth. She had kept this a secret from Donald until very recently. Until then, he had known that he was special, but not why.

The misery tree – how I help the bully

Kids activity

Fill in the spaces on the tree with the reasons.
Use feedback and anything else you can find.

1. I am different.

2. I jiggle like a tea bag.

3. I am shy.

4. I have poor eye contact.

5. I blush easily.

6. I am very sensitive.

7. I get angry back.

8. I am very nervous.

9. I am very intelligent.

10. I come from a different country/culture/religion.

11. I have learning difficulties.

12. I was in the wrong place at the wrong time.

13. I have no confidence.

14. I do nothing when bullied.

Some families pretend to the world – and themselves – that they are normal. They gloss over or minimise their own or their children's problems. They deny marital difficulties – 'It's none of their business' – or schoolwork problems – 'The teacher has a problem.' Although parents want to protect their child, their actions proclaim, 'I must protect you because you have problems'. Children aren't stupid: they identify the cover-up message and, as always, blame themselves, which lowers their self-confidence even further. If parents say, 'We deal with our problems at home', it teaches children to remain silent about problems, even bullying.

At home, children like to share their day, but secrets obstruct conversation. Likewise, keeping secrets at school – e.g. 'Our family is normal' – uses up a huge amount of a child's energy. It leaves no room for normal socialising. Secretive children who don't complain make good targets; they have limited energy to protect themselves from bullies, to build supportive friends and to report the bullying. Most families of bullies keep secrets about the level of abuse and neglect within their home, whether it is subtle or blatant. Then schools blame the bullies, who have copied their parents.

The 'special' child

Some families forget to acknowledge that they have a 'special' child, such as the child who was difficult to conceive, who barely survived birth, who was born after many miscarriages or the death of a sibling, or who is an only child, the 'baby', the first grandchild or the desired gender. Although the special child may have needed extra care earlier, later on she may still be overprotected. But the reason is kept secret, so she expects everyone to treat her as special, like her parents do. She makes a good target.

Family structures

One cannot blame children without looking at their families. Thus Genograms 1, 2 and 3 show three family structures. Although you don't know their socio-economic status, cultural background, environment, personalities, family history or anything else, their children are more likely to be a target. Conversely, Genograms 4 and 5 are more likely to have a child who bullies.

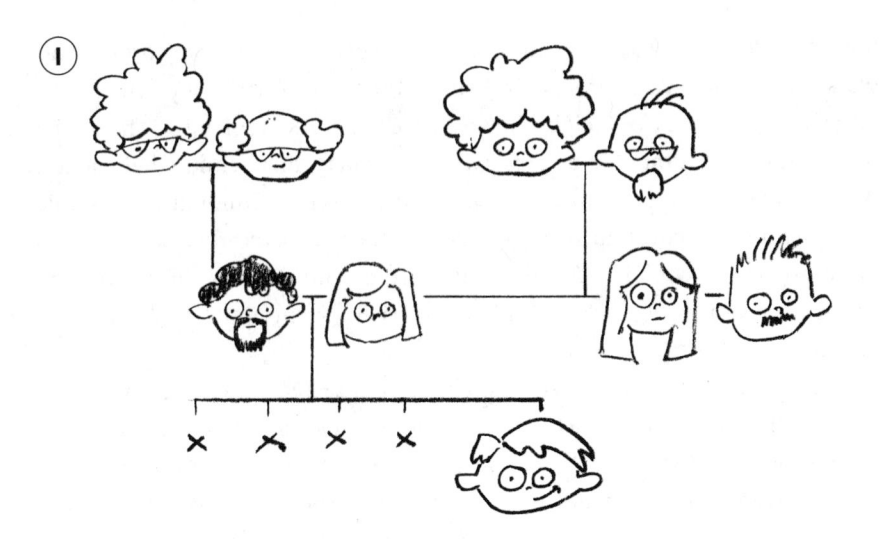

The above genogram shows a mother aged 38 and a father aged 45. The mother has had four miscarriages and their son was conceived through in-vitro fertilisation. Given the parents' ages and the miscarriages, it is unlikely they will have another child. Their son is the first and perhaps only grandchild for both families. He will be treated like a 'PIT' (prince-in-training) and mollycoddled by everyone, except bullies.

This genogram shows a mother aged 45 and a father aged 46. They have four children; the 'baby' was born eight years after the third child. Aged 10, he is a pseudo-adult with a 'big mouth' – he is spoilt and babied at home, and likely to be bullied at school.

The mother is aged 47. The child's father is somewhere, it doesn't matter where. He could be a sperm donor, divorced or away on business. The mother basically brings her daughter up on her own. The girl is aged 12 and is half-adult, half-child. She is like Mummy's little friend. She has little practice in socialising with her peer group. She is also an easy target for bullies.

(3)

Here is a family with Mother aged 43, Dad aged 46, and three kids aged 14, 15 and 16. Father is always yelling and fighting if anyone disagrees with him. Mother is passive and gives up. They disagree on all parenting matters, especially discipline. Some days big Jack (aged 14) can get away with attacking his sister (aged 15) and some days not. He makes a good school bully.

(4)

Here is a family where both parents work. Little Susie, aged nine, is cared for mainly by Grandma, who lives with the family. She is indulged, has no limits and gets away with everything. She is a sneaky bully at school: she 'sucks up' to teachers and bullies classmates.

Parents activity

Now draw your own genogram to explain why your child is being bullied or bullies.

School

You read in Chapter 3 that there are many reasons why schools perpetuate bullying. The school creates a culture that either accepts, condones or disapproves of bullying. This is reflected in its attitude to staff, parents and students. The school can either respect everyone or respect abuse and intolerance. When a school denies bullying, pretends to take action, punishes 'dobbing', leaves by-standers powerless or devalues staff and parents, it perpetuates bullying. No-one wins. When the school is led by a responsible principal who creates a consistent democratic structure, with rules and consequences and everyone getting a fair go, bullying is reduced.

Key points

- Understand the reasons for bullying to avoid blame and shame.
- Almost anyone can be targeted or can bully.
- There are many reasons why children are bullied or bully.

What to do

- When you understand the role your personality, family, past experiences, peers and school all play in the bullying, then you can take action.

10

Build your self-esteem – Secret 3

Everything you say and do, including your clothes and your voice, reflects the way you see yourself. If you feel good, you have true friends and your self-esteem is healthy. If your self-esteem is low, you attract difficult friends who manipulate, boss or bully you, which makes your self-esteem worse. Thus, the way your friends treat you is a reflection of the way you feel about yourself.

No-one can put you down except yourself!

If you have poor self-esteem, you feel bad about who you are. It's like having a bully living inside you. If you can't respect yourself, then you can't respect others; nor can they respect you. If your self-respect is low then it's hard to relate to all types of nice or nasty children. Basically, you let the bully relate to you in the same mean, critical way you relate to yourself.

Although some children believe it's acceptable to criticise themselves, they don't like others criticising them. They become angry! If you get upset and say, 'I'm not fat, you are!' or 'How dare you call me dumb!', the bully notices that you reacted to this tease but not to others. He will use it many times to bully you.

This is weird!

There's an odd paradox about blocking bullying: once you respect yourself, protect yourself and stop others bullying you, then some children start respecting you and want to be your friend!

Bullying destroys self-esteem

You have probably experienced a sinking feeling in your stomach following criticism, an attack, a put-down or a nasty remark. Some children have a thick skin and laugh it off, but you may experience it like an arrow through the heart. If you have been bullied or harassed for years, you will feel very bruised and battered. This lowers your self-esteem further: your social skills deteriorate, you withdraw from others, and other areas of your life, such as schoolwork or health, become problematic. A downward spiral is created.

The confidence game

You and your parents might believe that when you have the confidence, you can block bullies – but confidence comes when we are certain we can achieve. However, there are no guarantees that everything will work out as planned. What happens is that you decide to confront a challenge, e.g. learning a game. Once you learn the basic skills, you confront the next challenge to improve. True achievers are constantly reaching beyond their comfort zone. Each time they achieve their goal, they find another one to pursue. They are always extending themselves, learning new skills and operating in areas where they are unsure of success. Confidence is the last thing that most people talk about when contemplating a challenge; they use optimism and persistence instead.

Self-esteem shopping list

When a child gains confidence, his appearance often changes. How does a confident child appear?

- **Eyes:**   Firm gaze, like a cat on guard
- **Mouth:**   Relaxed, not tense like a yapping dog
- **Face:**   Calm expression, like a still pond

- **Body:** Flexible, like a jiggling tea bag
- **Shoulders:** Straight, like a coat-hanger
- **Chest:** Forward, unlike a deflated balloon
- **Arms:** Moving gracefully, unlike a nervous monkey
- **Legs:** Weight balanced, like a tightrope walker
- **Voice:** Firm, clear, steady, not like a crackly radio
- **Breathing:** Deep, like a dog relaxing
- **Coordination:** Like an athlete, not a newborn foal

How do *you* appear?

Fake it till you make it

Thus, looking for confidence is like looking for the pot of gold at the end of the rainbow. It is as elusive as looking for happiness. Once you begin looking, you will notice it trailing behind your shadow. You need to behave as if you already have confidence and positive self-esteem. It's not that hard to fool bullies – they usually aren't that alert or aware. Just pretend to be confident and 'fake it till you make it'. Imagine that you are being interviewed on television, and need to project a confident image. When you begin it may feel uncomfortable, but as you practise, as with learning any new skill, it will slowly come naturally.

That's not me!

Most kids know how to look confident sometimes, even if someone has to bribe them to do it. If someone asks you to change, you might say, 'But that's not me'. Well, who is it? You're not the same person at school as you are on holidays. If something wonderful or very awful happened to your family, you would be different, but you would still be you. Your body changes and renews itself constantly – hair, nails, skin, bones and all the other tissue. You regularly change your thoughts, likes and behaviour, depending on what is happening. And let's face it, if you were able to stop yourself being bullied, you would look and feel better immediately. But you would still be you.

The self-esteem bank

Self-esteem is like money in the bank. When you regularly deposit funds into your bank account, there is money when you need it. If you don't, there won't be enough funds when times are tough. Everyone has ups and downs. If your self-esteem bank is in credit, you can withdraw some to help you handle difficult, upsetting moments.

Good news story

Ian, a psychologist, lost his hair when he was six years of age. He was bullied for years. He explains: 'I learnt that by covering my head and always wearing caps, I was hiding from the real me and trying to become acceptable to others. This was a real burden.' After a while he stopped covering his head, and said, 'I needed to let them know that I was happy with the way I was. This put them at ease, and I also felt more at ease, instead of wondering how they would relate to me. The more I accepted myself, the more others accepted me.' He also laughed at himself and compensated by developing interesting hobbies.

Empower yourself with positive self-esteem

When you accept yourself as you are, including all your good and bad bits, your self-esteem is positive and productive. It means that you value your own needs and feelings before you can respect the needs and feelings of others. This doesn't mean that you are arrogant or 'up yourself', it just means that you are realistic and less vulnerable. Then you can give to others, obtain support, make friends and block bullies. If you feel good about yourself, you know that things will work out. You can laugh if someone hits a sensitive spot, and you can analyse the bully's game in order to take action.

Self-esteem boosters

In a perfect world, families, friends, classmates and teachers would provide you with self-esteem boosters. But this doesn't happen as often as you need it. Your parents may be the best in the world, but they get tired, busy or frustrated and forget to strengthen your self-esteem. Similarly, your friends may have other things on their minds. Your teachers can also be distracted by their responsibilities. You can't always expect self-esteem boosters from others – you need to provide yourself with your own collection of self-esteem boosters.

The three essential steps to good self-esteem

1. Give to yourself – build your self-esteem.

2. Allow others to give to you – feedback empowers.

3. Give to others – it boomerangs back to you.

1. Give to yourself – build your self-esteem

As you can't always rely on others, you need to give to yourself, not just once a week but every day. Then you can build up your self-esteem bank and feel good about yourself. There are many ways you can do this, but it can be as simple as playing with a toy, reading, listening to music or chatting to a friend.

Create your confidence-booster list

Kids activity

Find someone you trust. Ask him or her to help you discover what makes you feel confident, successful and powerful (e.g. doing well at sport, trying hard at schoolwork, cooking dinner for the family, riding your bike). Practise your confidence boosters as often as you can. If this isn't possible, then visualise yourself practising. Sometimes just thinking, dreaming and laughing about a confidence booster is enough for you to feel and act more positively. Write down your confidence-booster list.

....

....

....

Bossing your inner bully

Kids activity

Write down five bad (negative) things you do, say or think about yourself (e.g. I pick my nose, I write badly).

1...

2...

3...

4...

5...

Write down five good (positive) things you do, think or say about your- self (e.g. I write neatly, I keep my room tidy).

1...

2...

3...

4...

5...

Kids activity

Success stories

Write down some of your recent successes, including anything you said or did that required:

Courage (e.g. I walked past a mean-looking dog yesterday.)

....

Persistence (e.g. I learnt how to tie my shoelaces.)

....

Common sense (e.g. I told my mother about the bully.)

....

Good luck (e.g. The teacher happened to see the bully do it.)

....

Intuition (e.g. Mum loved the surprise cup of tea I made her.)

....

Problem solving (e.g. I worked out a tricky maths problem.)

....

Muscles (e.g. I opened the pickle jar when Grandma couldn't.)

....

Kids activity

Personal pep-talk

A pep-talk gives you a boost. Sports coaches motivate their teams with hyped-up pep-talks. Create your own pep-talks and write them on stickers. Put them everywhere – in your room, diary, bathroom, etc. – so you don't forget the message, e.g. 'I can do this', 'I'm not afraid', 'I like myself'.

Kids activity

Decorate the mirror

Every time you pass a mirror, practise smiling, blow yourself a kiss, give yourself a hug, use your pep-talk and practise looking confident (even if you have to 'fake it till you make it'!).

Kids activity

Make a 'feelgood' list

Write down three things you can do any time to make yourself feel good and improve your self-esteem. You can smell, touch, hear, taste, feel or imagine them (e.g. have a bubble bath, play a musical instrument, read, play with a pet, play sport).

1. ....

2. ....

3. ....

Now write down three things that make you feel good that you can take to school (e.g. little teddy, photo, special piece of inexpensive jewellery, gemstone, ball).

1. ....

2. ....

3. ....

Kids activity

Visualise the future

Find a nice spot to be alone, then relax and chill out. Empty your mind of bad thoughts and make room for good ones. Imagine yourself or someone else blocking the bully. Then ask yourself these questions:

- How will you feel when the bully looks stunned or embarrassed?

- How will you feel if the bully leaves you alone or wants to be your friend?

- What will you enjoy doing when you're not scared?

- What will be the fun parts of your life, e.g. your social life, schoolwork, health, weekends, etc.?

- What will be the best part of having true friends?

Kids activity

Be a fun person

Children with poor self-esteem aren't good at having fun. Friendly kids like having fun. If you are not fun to be with, they may exclude you and you'll feel worse. You need to smile and laugh more so that children enjoy being with you and think you're cool. Besides, laughing is a great way to get rid of tension, release painful feelings and feel better. To get in the mood for fun, complete these sentences:

- 'I am going to have more fun when I.............................'
  (e.g. tell jokes, smile more)

- 'I am going to laugh more when....................................'

- 'These kids are going to help me become more entertaining:

  ....,'

2. Allow others to give to you – feedback empowers

Tiffany believed in being natural. Unfortunately, the girls in her class didn't like her natural smell. They made snide comments behind her back and she often felt embarrassed. Eventually a kindly teacher took her aside and suggested that she wear a natural deodorant. The gossip stopped.

Science teaches us that for every action there is a reaction. Feedback is the response you receive to something you say or do. Some experts believe that there is no such thing as failure, only feedback. In other words, feedback is a learning experience.

There are different types of feedback:

- Positive, such as a compliment or praise. It makes you feel good, if you absorb it.

- Negative or critical, which can hurt, whether true or false. You may feel attacked and threatened, but it's actually more like a life-saving injection. It falls into three categories:

  - feedback which is totally untrue, e.g. 'You're ugly' (when you're attractive)

  - feedback which is true but said unkindly, e.g. 'You're dumb at maths' (nobody's perfect), and

  - feedback which is true but constructive, e.g. 'If you shut up in class, you'd hear the teacher telling us what to do' or 'When you stop interrupting, we'll listen to you' or 'Nobody likes a show-off' (the speakers are being sensible).

Feedback can be constructive and empowering or negative and disempowering. Everyone needs feedback to improve – can you imagine a top sportsperson surviving without a coach? Feedback helps us become the best at whatever we want to do, including dealing with bullies. Constructive feedback actually helps you improve what you do: your peers will become friendlier and you will block bullies. You will change and move on. When you receive feedback, enjoy the positive, learn from the constructive comments and trash the useless, untrue, unhelpful stuff.

Kids activity

Collect positive feedback

Jack had no friends. This made him more frustrated than he already was, so he'd fool around and make stupid comments in class. Everyone was sick of his attention-seeking behaviour: they retaliated by teasing him. His teacher gave him and his parents some constructive feedback. He then understood that if he wanted to make friends, he should be friendly, not stupid. The teasing stopped and his social life improved.

When someone smiles at or greets you, gives you a compliment, invites you to sit with them or join their game, contacts you at home or invites you to theirs, or does something which shows they value or respect you, then regard this gift as a positive self-esteem builder. You improve your self-esteem by requesting, observing and listening to feedback from lots of different people you respect – family and friends, teachers and peers; not just from your grandparents, who love you anyway – so that you get an accurate picture. Don't be shy about fishing for compliments! Then thank the person and save the feedback in your self-esteem bank. Write down gifts that you have received from your family, friends and others.

Today...

Yesterday...

Last week...

Another time...

BULLIES CAN BE RIGHT!

Kids called Anna a 'baby', so she asked them what she could do to be more mature. They didn't know. When she went home, she asked her older sister, who also called her a 'baby'. Her sister gave her some great ideas that worked!

When a bully teases you, don't get upset. Check if the tease is true but unkind or just untrue (see Chapter 5). If the bully is correct, it's free feedback. Then consider your options to deal with it: do you change the problem or accept it? Then move on. If the bully is wrong, gain his respect by giving a neutral retort. When kids call Lizzie an 'idiot', she says, 'I know, but I'm good at eating chocolate'.

Kids activity

Don't be a belly-button watcher

Lots of people give you gifts, but often you don't hear, see or feel the gift. Maybe you are so busy being a belly-button watcher (see Chapter 5) that you have less energy to absorb positive feedback from others. Then you ignore gifts which could rebuild your self-esteem. Write down some gifts you received but forgot to save!

1. ....

2. ....

3. ....

Who did you forget to thank for giving you a gift or a compliment in the past few days?

1. ....

2. ....

3. ....

TEACHER FEEDBACK

If teachers keep writing the same comments about you year after year, for example, 'Jenny does not participate enough in class' or 'Mark is very quiet' or 'Gina is not coping socially', this is constructive feedback. Or, they can give you or your parents feedback about your behaviours at school. This is valuable information because they won't say it unless it is something which needs to be improved.

Kids activity

Go shopping for constructive feedback

Claire had very long hair and a low fringe. No-one could see her face. All the other girls wore headbands and called her 'shaggy dog'. The moment she wore a headband and had her fringe cut, the teasing stopped.

Find children who can give you useful feedback and ask them:
'Could I have behaved differently?'
'Did I upset you when I...?'
'Why aren't you playing with me any more?'

Write down some negative, hurtful feedback that you trashed. Was it mean or constructive?

1. ....

2. ....

3. ....

Write down negative feedback that you have learnt from:

1. ....

2. ....

3. ....

3. Give to others – it boomerangs back to you

Another simple way of building your self-esteem is by giving to others. This works for lots of reasons. Kids like kids who like them. All children love special attention, especially if you show interest in their favourite subject – themselves. Once you do something to make someone else feel good, they are likely to return the compliment or favour and do something for you. When you are friendly, considerate and caring it can boomerang back to you. It may not happen immediately, but later on you will reap the benefits. At any school, everyone seems to know and respect the friendly, cheerful, generous children. They aren't bullied very often.

There are lots of ways you can give to children or adults. It may be as simple as smiling at five new people a day, helping a child with difficulties, or showing regular interest in someone else's hobbies, experiences or problems. If you help another child who is being bullied – e.g. by reporting to the teacher instead of doing nothing – or play with children who are alone, you can become a courageous kid.

Write down your gifts to others at school (e.g. chatted to the librarian, talked with a student from another class, complimented a child in your class). You may even try the same exercise at home with your family and see how you score.

Kids activity

Today...

Yesterday..

Last week...

Other times...

Tips for parents

Help your child rebuild his self-esteem so he has energy and confidence to block the bully and communicate at school.

Parents activity

- Enable him to improve the cause of the tease where possible, e.g. if the tease is about his hairstyle or uniform, help him change it. Or, if he can't play sport very well, help him practise.

- Be creative – place a note under his pillow or in his lunchbox; send a text message or email; praise your child in front of others.

- Encourage him to be more interesting, e.g. develop a hobby or special interest, learn the names of everyone in a team or a popular band.

- Enrol him in extra activities, e.g. Scouts, drama, holiday programmes.

- Play games to build confidence and social skills. Forget the electronic stuff – get out a ball, board game or cards and show him how to become a social winner or loser.

- Do things together, e.g. cooking, gardening, painting the classroom, camping – it builds self-esteem.

- Reward him with a gift or points towards a special treat, e.g. 'Each time you ring someone to make arrangements you'll get ten points toward the 50 you need for your special outing.'

- Pets (especially dogs) build self-esteem and teach children how to show care and empathy, and develop responsibility; they also provide exercise and allow kids to practise social skills at the park with other dogs and their owners.

- When you see your child displaying constructive assertive skills with a sibling, at camp or at a play rehearsal, remind him to repeat them elsewhere. Remind him that if he uses the behaviour successfully at home or elsewhere, he can duplicate it at school when appropriate, e.g. 'You speak loudly to your brother, so you can speak loudly to the bully next time you need to retort.'

- Use feedback to praise your child. Children need praise like a plant needs water. Children who are regularly praised by their families have better self-esteem. Praise their assertive behaviours to them and to others (like grandparents, siblings), e.g.:

  'I'm really impressed that you looked those girls straight in the eye.'
  'You smiled at more people today, that's great.'
  'I'm pleased you are speaking to more kids.'
  'I'm glad you tried a retort, even if it didn't work this time.'

Check that they absorbed the compliment, to ensure it didn't go in one ear and out the other. When you praise them for doing a chore, behaving nicely or developing assertive skills, how do you know they've actually heard you? Did they smile and look pleased? Did their face glow? Did they sit or stand a little taller?

Kids appear to automatically switch off when their parents speak, unless it's about a treat. If their behaviour doesn't change, your praise may have fallen on deaf ears, and it won't work. You could repeat yourself until you get the correct response, or ask them in a humorous manner to repeat back to you what they heard you say.

Instruct your child how to behave when receiving a compliment, i.e. a genuine smile, a snappy jerk of the head or a generally cheerful, contented demeanour. If you see your child displaying the appropriate behaviour, point this out to him and show him how he did it.

Key points

- Children need to build their self-esteem to block bullies. They do this by giving to themselves and to others.
- Children with good self-esteem show it, and attract real friends.
- Children need to use positive and constructive feedback.
- Adults need to actively contribute to enhancing a child's self-esteem.

What to do

- Help yourself feel good by doing nice things for yourself everyday.
- Listen carefully when others say or do nice things for you.

11

Become a confident communicator – Secret 4

Remember when your teacher was away and a relief teacher came to your class? The moment he or she stood in the doorway, everyone knew what would happen next: if the teacher stood there looking nervous and insecure, you knew this would be a slack lesson, with kids messing around. But when the teacher stood upright, eyes fixed on the class, radiating control, you realised there wouldn't be any playing-up in class today.

You communicate what you think, feel and want through your behaviours. You judge a person by the way she communicates, from the smiles, nods and warm laughter of friends to the raised eyebrow, stunned gasp or shout of stressful encounters.

Children with good communication skills can relate to different types of people, in friendly and challenging situations. They connect socially and defuse conflict. They say what they mean and their body language reflects their words. Their message is clear. If they're feeling good, they sound cool. If they're angry, they're furious! They're generally the popular children.

If you are being bullied, you are doing something to advertise your vulnerability. You look like limp celery, your eyes jiggle like a tea bag and your voice is muffled. You either plead, 'Don't bully me,' or you threaten back. The average bully won't respect you and continues her game. Shyness, secrecy and sarcasm are poor communication skills others don't know what you think and feel, so your friends do nothing to help. You need to change so that other children like you and help you.

Alternatively, if you are using bullying behaviours, you show that you need to be in control and expect to be obeyed. You attract false, temporary friends who suck up to you to be safe, and then gossip behind your back. You risk payback. Once you learn how to communicate with respect and empathy, you will attract genuine friendships.

The communication game

The main communication skills involve eyes, face, body language, voice (breathing) and words. The bulk of successful communication is physical (nonverbal) – only a small percentage involves words:

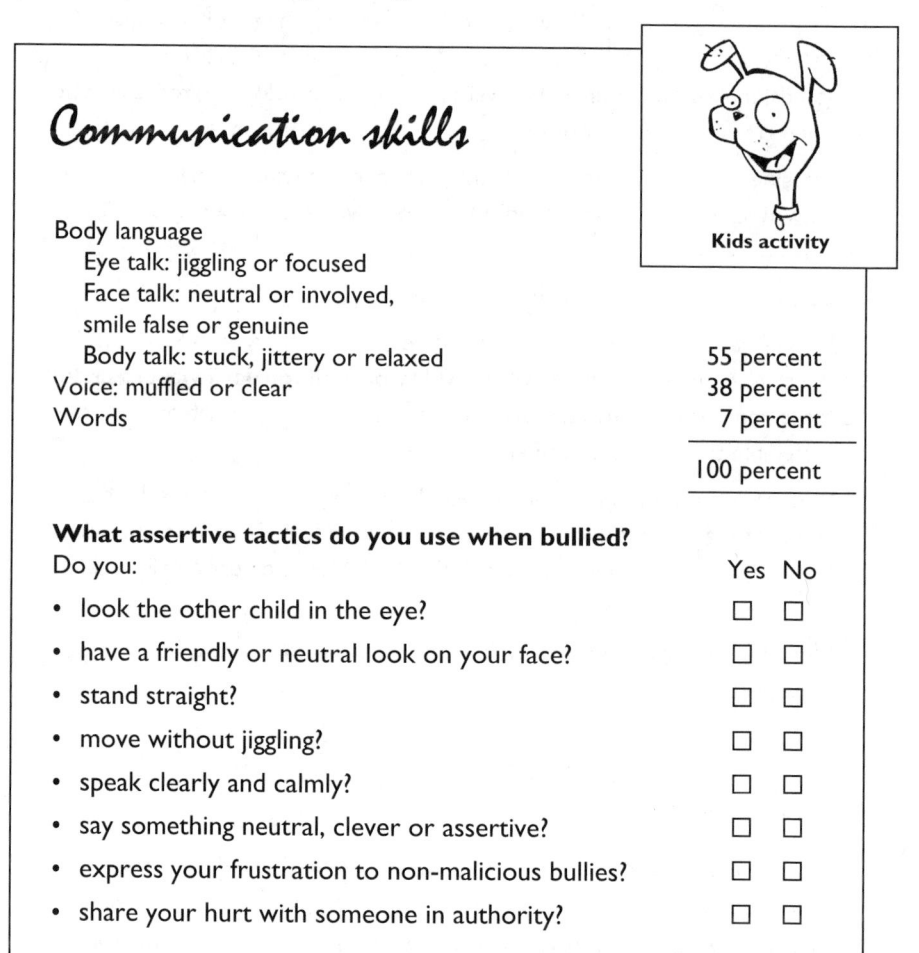

Communication skills

Body language
    Eye talk: jiggling or focused
    Face talk: neutral or involved,
    smile false or genuine
    Body talk: stuck, jittery or relaxed   55 percent
Voice: muffled or clear   38 percent
Words   7 percent

     100 percent

Kids activity

What assertive tactics do you use when bullied?
Do you: Yes   No

- look the other child in the eye?   ☐   ☐
- have a friendly or neutral look on your face?   ☐   ☐
- stand straight?   ☐   ☐
- move without jiggling?   ☐   ☐
- speak clearly and calmly?   ☐   ☐
- say something neutral, clever or assertive?   ☐   ☐
- express your frustration to non-malicious bullies?   ☐   ☐
- share your hurt with someone in authority?   ☐   ☐

First impressions

Most kids judge each other in the first four seconds! (Dogs take even less time.) This is the survival instinct in action. As the bully will judge you very quickly, you need to look confident to block him – even if you don't feel confident. Imagine that it's the same as getting dressed to play sport or go to a party: nobody wants to see a nervous footballer or a frightened party-goer.

Parents activity

Instant confidence

Most of the kids I've tried this exercise with have lots of fun with it.

Give your child a nursery rhyme or a simple story. Ask him to read or recite it. Watch how he looks, stands, moves and sounds. He will probably behave like melted chocolate. Then give these instructions:

'Imagine you are the most confident person in the whole world! How would you look and stand? How would you move your body? How would you sound and behave?'

Can you see a difference in his behaviour?

'Now I want you to repeat the same nursery rhyme/story as though you were the most confident kid in the whole wide world.' (If you don't want to say 'the most confident kid in the world', ask him to imagine describing something incredible to a television camera.)

Most children stand up suddenly, head high, eyes up, shoulders straightened, voice stronger – and they look much more confident. Then, when they finish the nursery rhyme, they slump back to their previous posture, like limp celery!

Most children know how to look confident. Now say, 'I know you can do it, now do it around bullies.'

Be a copy-cat

Aaron, aged 14, was different to his classmates. He looked, sounded and behaved differently. He eventually worked out how to look like them. He began dressing like them (his shirt hung out), sat next to them at lunchtime, and talked about sport (like most boys do). His advice: 'If you don't have the confidence to stand out, find ways to blend in with your peers or you could look like a target.'

You can copy the way popular, assertive children behave in social and difficult situations. Check the feedback to make sure you are improving. Look at movies and television shows to see how confident people behave: observe their appearance, clothes, hairstyle, voice, body language and ability to confront bullies.

Look cool!

If you want to belong to a certain tribe, you need the appropriate communication skills, clothes and accessories for membership. Children use jewellery, a mobile phone, and so on to express their personality and their connection to their group. Popular kids wear the latest fashion in a special way while nerds go for an old-fashioned/homemade/unkempt look. It's harder to feel confident if you are different: other kids may not welcome you into their group.

So, regardless of whether you wear a uniform or casual clothing to school, your clothes, schoolbag, lunchbox, pencil case, glasses, deodorant, shoes, socks, hairstyle, etc. should identify who you are and allow you to blend in. They don't need to be expensive – you can shop for designer copies at a market or a charity shop or thrift store. If you have religious dress requirements, blend in where possible. You could copy the popular kids or ask some nice, friendly kids for feedback, but don't break any school rules. When you look trendier, you feel more confident and look like you 'belong'.

Kids activity

How do you look?

	OK (trendy)	Not OK (nerdy)
Glasses	☐	☐
School clothes/uniform	☐	☐
Hemlength	☐	☐
Shirt/T-shirt	☐	☐
Jeans/pants	☐	☐
Shoes	☐	☐
Jewellery/watch	☐	☐
Schoolbag	☐	☐
Pencilcase	☐	☐
Diary	☐	☐

What needs changing?...

Practice techniques

There are lots of ways to help you learn communication skills:

- The quickest way is to video yourself for a few minutes, then replay and discuss with an adult. It's easy to see what needs changing. It may be uncomfortable but the result is worth it. Continue until you are successful. If you don't own a video camera, borrow one from school or elsewhere for a session.

- Alternatively, get an adult to mirror exactly what you say and do, then discuss it afterwards.

- Get someone to help you role-play. Check your eye contact, face talk, voice and body talk. Do you sound serious or friendly, assertive, passive or aggressive?

- Try out the skills with dolls, soft toys or puppets.

- Keep a record of your new, improved skills, e.g. smiling more, speaking louder.

- Get someone to take 'before' and 'after' photos of how you smile, stand and move while you aren't aware.

- Practise communication skills every day.

Reward small changes

Acknowledge, reward and praise any new, assertive behaviour, even if it is a tiny step in the right direction. For example, reward the girl who smiles when she relates a positive move, or the boy who sounds less miserable than he did the day before. When they do it naturally, point it out. Here are some examples:

Parents activity

eye contact, a real smile, being friendly to other children, sitting quietly (not shuffling their feet), and being empathic to a schoolmate.

Nonverbal power skills

Animals don't rely upon words – they use sounds and nonverbal body language to communicate with one another and demonstrate their tribal status. Similarly, your power can come from using assertive body language.

'Eye talk'

Strong eye contact is a basic survival skill for all human and other beings. Have you seen a cat stare a dog away? Eye contact allows you to instantaneously assess everyone you meet, to see if they are nice or not nice. It connects you to friendly beings and protects you from nasty ones. In Western society it involves looking the other person straight in the eye: eyeball to eyeball, or 'eye talk'. If you find eye contact difficult, it advertises your vulnerability.

Once you establish proper eye contact, you automatically stand straighter, breathe more oxygen and become less anxious. Your voice has more room to resonate in your chest, so you sound louder. You look more confident. If eye contact is unacceptable in your culture, then find out what else you can do to check out who is friendly and who is not, and how to feel safe e.g. check hand movements – are they relaxed (nice) or tense (nasty)? You need to practise until you can do this naturally.

SOME DON'TS:

- Don't stare at the ground.

- Don't jiggle your eyes like a tea bag, unless you use them like a searchlight to stare at mean kids. Many targets move their eyes around a lot instead of focusing on the bully – eye to eye. This demonstrates vulnerability.

- Don't allow glasses to disguise your message. Show your power in other ways e.g. stand very tall, use strong arm movements, speak louder, emphasise certain words.

Parents and kids activity

Finger exercise for jigglers

I use this exercise often with kids – they love it.

Every time your child shares something significant – about her day, an outing, friends – get her to face you and check her eye contact. If her eyes are jiggling like a tea bag, tell her that you will follow her eyes with your finger while she is talking. (You can even draw a face on your finger.) Once she begins speaking, follow her eyes with your finger. Most children find this distracting but amusing. It's a great way to learn about the necessity for eye contact. Practise this regularly until she does it. Instruct others to request eye contact, e.g.

family, teachers, neighbours. If your child forgets, just hold up your finger and follow her eyes around. She will remember and laugh!

SOME 'EYE-DEAS'

- Focus on a point between the bully's eyes. Pretend that your eyes are lasers. Then emit a beam which drills right through the bully.

- Create a variety of stares, for example, a curious stare, a blank stare, an aggressive one, and absolute amazement.

- Find your warning or 'watch out' look – in other words, 'You mess with me and I'll take action'. (I am sure you have one at home.)

- You may prefer to look spaced out, bored or tired.

- You could focus your eyes on something else, like blowing bubblegum, taking notes or filing your nails.

Face talk

Your face is like the instrument panel of a plane. It has hundreds of fine muscles which communicate what you think and feel. You use them to make friends and socialise with your family and other nice people. When they know what you think and feel, they can trust you with their thoughts and feelings. If you don't express yourself, you will be shy and lonely because most people don't bother using guessing games to socialise. You also need the fine muscles of your face to show your fear and frustration and to ask for help.

SMILES AND SMIRKS

The smile is a sign of being friendly and relaxed. It brings more blood to the brain and helps you think and feel better. Some children, especially shy ones, can't smile very well. Their timid, tense lips reveal an attitude, giving them a silly smile or smirk. When dealing with bullies, you need a neutral mouth or a relaxed smile. Practise until you can do it properly and naturally.

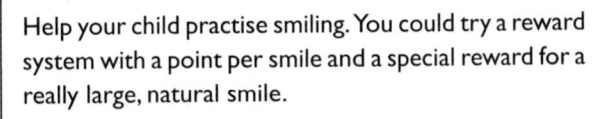

Help your child practise smiling. You could try a reward system with a point per smile and a special reward for a really large, natural smile.

Parents and kids activity

BLANK OUT YOUR FACE

Although you need to show what you think and feel on your face with most people, including mean friends, when you are dealing with very nasty bullies (e.g. saltwater crocodiles), this will make them happy. Instead, you have to wear a pleasant, blank, neutral mask. Then the bully won't know what you are feeling inside. (It's none of her business, is it?) Don't look sad, mad or bad. Besides, most kids are good at looking blank when they want to avoid trouble, e.g. when a teacher catches them talking at the wrong time.

You can train the muscles of your face to be neutral (with nasty bullies) or animated (for family and friends), depending on the situation. You need to work out how to relax your eyes, jaw and cheeks. Your lips can't be floppy or rigid, but can be manipulated to deliver a clear, firm, assertive message.

Giving blank looks

Help your child regularly practise a pleasant, plain face. Use a phrase to trigger the right mood, e.g. 'I'm a couch potato', 'I'm a cloud' or 'I'm a cat in the sun'. A good time to practise is after a meal, when she is relaxed. Help her do it naturally and automatically.

Parents activity

Body talk

Have you ever seen a teacher striding confidently down a corridor? Similarly, athletes and dancers value each movement they make, and entertainers sense the impact of their behaviour on their audience, like a singer who claps his hands in the air to get you to clap. Confident animals appear relaxed and move steadily, whereas a frightened animal shows fear by its frenzied behaviour.

When you look like a scared rabbit or a floppy doll, you make a good target. The bully observes your fear and anger in your body movements. If you have been bullied, you look uptight, you don't breathe deeply and your head is crooked as though it's about to fall off. You need to change your body movements so that the bully can't identify your feelings. Once you control your movements, you can look confident.

- Stand or sit upright and proud. Don't be rigid like a soldier, but supple like an athlete or dancer.

- Pretend that someone has attached a string to the top of your head and is pulling you up. Don't behave like a curvy banana or wobbly octopus, stand tall like a giraffe.

- Practise planting your feet about 30 cms apart, look the bully in the eye and say something assertive, e.g. 'I'm tired of your comments about my face, next week I want something else' or 'Thanks for the feedback'.

- Check how you use your fingers, hands, arms and legs. Don't make sudden or jerky body movements.

- Practise walking with a confident posture for five minutes every day. Get an adult to give feedback.

The tea bag trick

Children don't know how they appear to other children. Does your child move around a lot? Can't sit or stand still? Do her arms and legs wiggle like an octopus?

Parents activity

If so, get a tea bag. Every time your child wriggles, jiggle the tea bag. She'll laugh and get the message.

CHECK YOUR BODY SPACE

Space determines our relationship to someone else. (Australians like lots of space, Asians often like to be close.) Like a cat, you can use space to regulate your behaviour. Find out the local optimal distance for relating to and blocking a bully. You can move closer to the bully or further away. Imagine standing extremely close to the bully and saying, 'I'm quite deaf, say that louder' or 'Can I look at your pupils?'. Instead of bending towards the bully, you could bend a little backwards, which shows that you are uninterested and less scared.

Visualisation – a great tool to change body language

- Pretend there is a thick, tall, glass wall between you and the bully that blocks the bully's vibes.

- Imagine you are enclosed in a huge plastic balloon. When the bully comes near, move away in case she damages your balloon.

- Transform the bully into a mosquito. Spray her with a venomous look to paralyse her temporarily.

- Use a 'bully button': Jack had one in the middle of his forehead which he pressed to start his automatic replies. Or use your belly-button instead.

- The moment someone is mean to you, listen to your gut feelings and protect yourself.

COPY AND CONVERT THE BULLY

Bullies like to show their power. If they use threatening body language, stand up straight and stare. If the bully is shouting, be loud and noisy but not aggressive. If the bully is bantering and joking at your expense, laugh loudly and dramatically with her. Once you have copied the bully's behaviour, lower your energy level to a more comfortable one. Bullies may follow your example and lower theirs.

You can change the bullying game by breaking your pattern and doing something unexpected, e.g. look blank, scratch yourself, cough loudly, appear to vomit, or offer the bully a chewy toffee that jams her jaws shut. The game alters when the bully realises that you are not upset or powerless. She usually stops.

Parents and kids activity

Body language collage

This is a simple exercise for a young child. Get a pair of children's scissors, glue, paper and lots of magazine pictures. Ask your child to cut and paste children who look assertive: standing up, sitting down, walking or playing sport, alone or with other children. Help your child identify what they do to look confident.

Body check

If you look like a:

- limp celery
- frightened rabbit
- frozen ice-block
- miserable mess
- jiggling tea bag
- couch potato
- wriggling octopus, or
- prickly echidna,

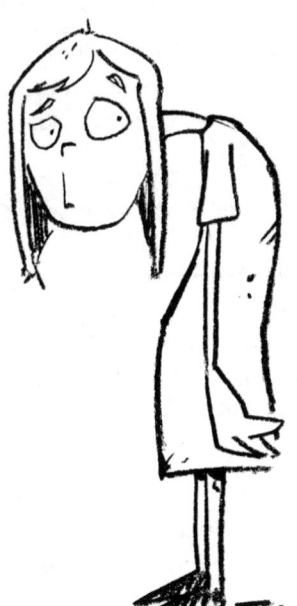

you need to:

- be confident like a lion
- behave like a martial-arts expert
- speak like an actor
- repel like a prickly rose bush
- stand like a horse
- move like an athlete
- joke like a comedian, and
- copy popular kids

If you say it's hard, then remember:

- fake it till you make it
- practice makes it natural
- you will be the same but happier
- give it a go and know when to say 'No!'
- success means persistence, and
- don't make the bully happy.

Breathing

When you are relaxed, you breathe deeply and slowly. When you are scared or angry, your breathing becomes shallow and your breathing pattern is irregular. Bullies, like dogs, sense your pattern of breathing in order to protect themselves. You need to improve your breathing to look relaxed. Then you will also have a stronger, clearer voice to say what you need to say.

Kids activity

Breath energiser

Relax yourself. Then breathe in and out a few times. Shift your attention from your nose to the centre of your body, around your belly-button. Then breathe in and out from there. This is a deeper breath and takes longer to inhale and exhale. Continue breathing, and imagine there is a great pool of energy flowing from your centre. Visualise the energy expanding and increasing. Feel the energy as it rises and flows through your body and out through your toes, head and fingertips. Now imagine that it is flowing outside your body, creating a barrier of energy all around you. Don't be distracted by the bully – let the 'energy block' protect you.

Your voice is your transmitter

Animals mainly understand the tone of your voice, not your words. Your voice establishes who you are. Just as your accent shows your origins, a mumble reflects fear. Children know whether to respect or to bully you. If you have a babyish voice, they won't respect you. If your voice is animated, you are seen as assertive.

You should sound calm, natural and relaxed, as though you are talking about the weather or are at home with your family. The trick is to focus on your breathing – slow and deep – to stay calm. Alternatively, you can use silence to create a space between you and others: just stop, wait, and wait, which forces them to act.

SPEAK LOUDLY

- Do others keep asking you to repeat yourself? Shy kids speak very quietly. It's no use learning a great retort that nobody hears.

- If you have a boring voice (get feedback), then be loud. The bullies will think you are less scared.

- You might say 'Stop it!' in your best 'Grade Three teacher' voice, or shout in front of a group, 'When will you stop bullying me?'

SPEAK CLEARLY

Mumbling is no good: you run the risk of sounding passive or passive-aggressive. Speak clearly so that your friends, family and the bully understand the words you use and what you want.

- Practise sounding clear, firm and assertive.

- Try whispering with a smile on your face, while moving up very close to a bully. This will look assertive.

Parents and kids activity

Help your child change her quiet voice

- Use video camera playback.

- Record her speaking loudly to siblings.

- Tell her to speak like she does on a mobile phone.

- Take her to a voice coach or a speech teacher, or to drama lessons.

Voice power

This simple exercise demonstrates voice power. Ask your child to read each sentence eight times, stressing a different word each time:

I did not say he kicked my leg.
I did not say she took my book.

Show her how stressing each word creates a different meaning and changes the message.

GENDER TALK

There are many differences between the way boys and girls communicate. This is influenced by your culture and your family traditions. Regardless of your gender, you need to learn how to say what you think, feel and want.

- Girls often mention things and hope the listener will understand by implication or intuition. They have good verbal skills and can discuss a number of things at the same time. They notice detail and are more sensitive. They tend to be better at sharing their feelings and seeking closeness with others in small groups. Girls tend to hope that others will notice their plight and rescue them.

- Boys like to make a point and expect to be heard. They tend to focus on one subject at a time. Most boys find it difficult to identify their feelings. They tend to 'bottle and retreat', or 'bottle and burst'. Males are more competitive: even when they socialise, they compete by showing what they know or have achieved. They hang around in larger groups. Their verbal skills are less developed than girls until some time after puberty. They can find it difficult to verbalise their feelings to protect themselves. Boys escape to their cave (or computer) when threatened.

Verbal power skills

Your words represent your current state of mind. They reflect your mood by broadcasting each of your thoughts and feelings. Thus, they are communication tools that you need to use with care to empower yourself.

Be yourself

- If you can't hear your own inner voice, you can't listen to others.

- Listen to your gut feelings – they are usually right.

- Trust your guts and say what you mean.

- Say it like you mean it – match your feelings to your words.

- Say what you think, feel and want – nobody can guess what's in your mind.

- When it's too hard to fake being nice, then be real.

- Children respect children who are honest.

Avoid blank-out moments

Sometimes, when someone asks a question, you feel so overwhelmed, confused or anxious that you become silent. The other child will think that you're stupid or not interested. Instead, work out what to say, e.g. 'Pardon?', 'I don't know', 'What do you mean by that?', 'I don't understand', 'My brain has gone to sleep', 'I can't remember'.

Use connecting statements

Sometimes it's hard to know what to say even though you want to show your interest in the conversation. The use of connecting statements depends on where you live and your peer group. You can learn them by watching television or by listening to other kids. Listen for common lingo and slang expressions at your school, e.g. 'Awesome, like, man, cool, wow, yeah...', 'Well, mate...', 'Gee whiz', 'Sounds yummy', 'And then what happened?'. And make sure you indicate your full attention by doing a 'noddy' (i.e. nodding like a television interviewer).

'Gut talk' – the magic 'I' word

The 'I' word is the basis of assertive language, or 'gut talk'. It looks really simple, but very few people use it successfully at home, at school or socially. This type of language doesn't blame, attack or make anyone defensive. You just take responsibility for what you think, feel and say. Just compare 'It's nice being with you' to 'I like being with you'; or 'You shouldn't interrupt' to 'I don't like you interrupting me'.

Assertive language forces the other person to provide you with instant feedback. You can find out whether he cares about what you feel or not. You actually make him accountable. For example:

'*I feel that...*'

'I feel that you are being mean to me when you leave me out.'

'I feel very angry about the way the kids spread rumours about me.'

'I am upset because kids tease me.'

'I feel upset when you call me an idiot.'

You need to share your feelings if you want to socialise and stop being bullied. If you are scared of upsetting a friend, you prolong your agony by being friendly to someone who doesn't really care for you. Alternatively, some kids tease for fun; they don't realise that they have gone too far and have hurt your feelings. You will find that if the kid cares, he'll feel bad, say sorry and stop. If he doesn't care, he will continue. As a general rule, don't express your pain to the bully. It will make him happy. Instead, use a cool, neutral voice with a bully or a mean friend and tell him what you think and what you will do:

'*I think that...*'

'I think that name-calling is a form of bullying. If you don't stop I will report you.'

'I think it's unfair. I've done most of the project and you have been slacking.'

'I think that those boys are excluding me.'

You need to trash any faulty beliefs and attitudes and work out your thoughts. Then you can decide what to say to the bully and what to discuss with significant adults at home or school. You need to tell your friends and others what help you require:

'*I would like you to...*'

'I would like you to stop pushing me around.'

'I want you to behave like a true friend; if not, then forget it.'

'I don't want to give that to you.' (repeat like a broken record)

'Mum/Dad, I'd like you to speak to the principal because the teacher can't help.'

'Teacher, I would like you to tell those kids to stop attacking me.'

Action talk

Many children don't know how to be friendly, to make and keep friends. This means that you don't choose true friends. When you need friends, they've disappeared or do nothing. Besides, when you have friends, even if they are a bunch of 'nerds', you are less likely to be targeted because you belong to a group and you're not a loner.

Using feedback as your guide, use this simple recipe:

- Ask questions – prepare five for girls and five for boys, e.g. about sport, shopping, music, weekends. Just ask the question and do some 'noddies'. They will think you are being friendly.

- Chat – talking about simple, everyday things builds trust.

- Show interest – people like people who like them and who are like them. You can still show interest even though it's not your thing – television presenters do it all the time. Listen carefully and make connecting statements to show you are connected to them.

- Share empathy – this builds a real connection and is the basis of caring friendships. Friends show real care for one another and say what they think, feel and want.

- Deal with feedback and conflict – everyone has different ideas. Even friends need to discuss, negotiate and find a resolution. When you express your opinion, you get equal power and you block bullying.

- Plan – 'Let's do…'. You need to make arrangements and spend time regularly with friends, either on the phone, via the Internet or in person to build a friendship.

Parents and kids activity

Practise 'I' statements at home

Ask your child to tell you how he is feeling about something that is upsetting him. Reply in a way that provides him with practice in dealing with people who care and people who don't care. Here are some examples:

Child:	'Mum, I'm angry that you forgot to wash my sports clothes.'
Adult:	'I know that you are annoyed, but I warned you last week that this would happen if you didn't do your chores.'
Child:	'Everybody is going away for the holidays. Why can't we go somewhere?'
Adult:	'I would love to go away, too, but we can't afford it this year.'

Child:	'I feel very bad when you yell at me.'
Adult (caring):	'I didn't know. You never told me before.'
Adult (non-caring):	'So what, I'm in a bad mood.'

Kids activity

Write down five skills that you need to practise to become friendly, fun, cool and confident.

1. ....

2. ....

3. ....

4. ....

5. ....

Parents activity

Table talk

Get the family to sit around the dinner table at meal times. Table talk is one of the best ways to encourage your child to develop communication skills, share what is happening, and plan action. Give everyone the opportunity to talk.

- Don't ask, 'How was school today?' Ask who he played with at lunch or recess, or what he did. Find out if anything funny or good happened or if he's stressed or upset about something.

- Regularly invite others to join you and provide your child with more table-talk practice.

- If your child's other parent lives elsewhere, encourage them to meet for a meal regularly.

- Give your child the opportunity to challenge you with his beliefs or about something he wants changed, such as homework, chores or privileges. Encourage him to argue, debate and negotiate a resolution with you.

Key points

- Effective communication skills block bullying and help you make more friends.
- Communication skills involve your eyes, face, body language, voice and words.

What to do

- Get help to project a positive, confident image – don't be scared, be prepared.
- Practise assertive communication skills.
- Look for small changes in behaviour.

12

Create your own 'power pack' – Secret 5

Dallas is terrified that kids will tease him about his father being blind, and criti-cise his dad's guide dog. We played around with some ideas and practised until he felt prepared. Now if someone teases him he can say, 'Well, my dad is a very intelligent man. He has a great life and career, and he is a really lovely man. Gary, the dog, is very intelligent because he has passed Stage 5 of guide-dog school, which is very difficult.' If kids tease Dallas that he too might become blind, he can say, 'Who knows what the future will be? I don't.'

You need to protect yourself from mean, nasty and abusive people wherever they are – at home, school, or later at work. Besides, children don't respect 'nice' children – they respect children who are genuine, who stand up for themselves, speak their mind and say what they feel; children who don't put up with uncom-fortable, stressful or abusive behaviours; who don't inflame a difficult situation, but defuse it. They are the popular ones. Everyone wants to be their friend! When you use assertive, self-protective behaviours, most bullies back off and respect you. In fact, dealing with stressful encounters and bullying is part of any relation-ship. It is an essential social survival skill.

This chapter will provide you with many ideas for dealing with teasing, exclusion, physical bullying and harassment. These ideas can give you a smile or activate you. Remember that bullies love secrecy and hate publicity.

The main types of teasing

Children use three levels of words. These depend on your culture, language, the school and your community. Although some words seem meaningless, they may carry a nasty connotation at your school.

Level 1: These are the words you may find easier to share with your parents and teachers:

- dumb, imbecile, dummy, weak, moron, idiot, loser, bimbo, mental

- dork, wuss, dag, nerd, square, geek, wimp

- shortie, shrimp, unco(ordinated), spaso (spastic), fatso, four eyes, tram tracks, retard, freckle face, feral, girl, surfboard (flat-chested), pindick (small penis)

- sook, hopeless, pest, nuisance, pathetic, baby, crybaby, shut up

- you smell, go away, I don't want to catch your germs, germinated

Level 2: This list usually includes swear words. You know they are bad words because you look anxious, ashamed or embarrassed; you blush, squirm, jiggle, lower your head and avoid eye contact. You don't like telling them to adults. These are the hidden words that most bullies use:

- ching-chong boy, wog, dago, slant-eye, Jew, monkey (people with dark skin), dog (to a Muslim), city snob, mainlander, peasant.

- dickhead, wanker, little dick

- bullshitter, arsehole, fart face, pile of shit/poo/diarrhoea, shithead

- bitch, bitch lips, bastard, slut, prostitute

- homosexual, homo, poofter, (leso) lesbian, gay

- your mother is... (never your father).

Level 3: These words are the worst: although most primary-age children hear them at school, they are scared to tell adults. These words elicit the greatest amount of sensitivity, a stunned silence or anger from adults who deny them, or hilarity when children and adults laugh while releasing pent-up, painful feelings about bullying. These are the 'f' word and the 'c' word, e.g.:

- fucking bitch, fuck face, fuckwit, fuck you, fuck off, fuck your mother

- fucking cunt, you're a cunt, cuntface.

Past and present teases

Write down the names you've been called:

Kids activity

....

....

....

Strip the tease

- The bully scores each time you become upset and then react.

- Decide whether the tease is true or not.

- If it's not true, why get upset?

- If it is true, why get upset? Maybe you can change, e.g. lose weight, practise sport, change hairstyles.

- What can you do to accept a permanent situation, such as a physical disability, your ethnicity – e.g. make a joke or a fun limerick, get a confidence badge? Whatever it is, circulate a detailed leaflet about your condition in your class.

- Ask an adult for help.

- Get energy by de-sensitising and defusing mean words on the tease list until they are less painful, e.g. The bully said, 'Bitch'. Retort: 'How can you be a bitch when you're not a dog?'

The bully said, 'Smart-arse'. Retort: 'How can you be a smart-arse when bottoms don't have a brain?'

- Play word games with similar letters or meaning, e.g. bully – bulldozer, bullish, bulletproof, bulldog.

- Beware that your retort doesn't have to be related to the tease, e.g. 'You're dumb'; reply: 'And I like football.'

- Find ways to re-frame or re-label, e.g. 'No, I'm intellectually challenged/horizontally enhanced/conversationally selective', etc.

- The bully said, 'You are a... [migrant].' Retort: 'Yes, we came from... [Siberia, Nerdsville, Geekland] and our traditions make your country multicultural' or, 'Everybody in America is a migrant except the native Americans.'

- The bully said, 'You're a Jew/Muslim, etc....' Reply: 'I feel good about that because we have yummy foods and great presents.'

- Share something important with the bully that she can identify with, such as your customs, food, music, culture, e.g. 'Did you know that Jewish merchants brought Chinese pasta to Italy?', 'Did you know that India invented the zero?', 'Did you know that...?'

Parents activity

How to best help your child

- Switch off your own feelings in order to empower your child.

- Allow your child to challenge you sometimes.

- Do a stocktake of all the bullying, including swear words.

- Beware if a child says, 'I don't care'. She does, otherwise she wouldn't say it.

- Friend or foe? Help your child distinguish between friendly fools or bully bitches/bastards.

- Help your child disguise or de-sensitise her pain, anger and fear in order to take action.

- Don't blame the bully. Children should respond, not retaliate.

Action checklist for kids

- *Act assertive*: Use strong eye contact, a neutral, blank face, good posture, a clear strong voice and assertive body movements with mean kids.

- *Be cool*: It doesn't matter what you say as long as you look, sound and behave as though you are calm, confident, polite and respectful. Then you use your power to force the bully to back off.

- *Get comfortable*: Find something neutral, non-threatening and comfortable to say. You can use a short reply like 'Fancy that' or a longer retort.

- *'Talk to the hand'*: This African–American expression means that no-one is listening. It comes with its own locally accepted hand and body movements. It is often used in movies, and is generally non-threatening.

- *Don't retaliate*: There is no need to be rude, aggressive, sarcastic, etc. That's like fanning a fire. If you show frustration, the bully knows she has scored a hit.

- *Be honest*: Don't lie and say 'Everything is fine' or 'I don't care what you say' when you don't mean it. The bully knows you do. If it's safe, express your feelings, e.g. 'I am really hurt that you said…' or 'I don't like what you are doing'.

- *Stay safe*: Don't show your feelings if it's not safe. It's none of the bully's business what you feel, is it? Don't make her happy, just disguise or release your feelings.

- *Make a joke*: e.g. 'It's not good for your reputation to be seen with a nerd like me' or 'If you stand too close, you'll catch my germs' or 'I don't want you getting into trouble, so stop being mean'.

- *Get in first*: If you make fun of yourself, you frustrate bullies who want to make you look bad. A boy I know believes that by saying it first, it showed that he didn't care and it took away their power. He made it hard for them to upset him. They gave up.

- *Have target practice*: Ask your parents, sibling(s), cousin, friend or teacher to coach you for five minutes every night. Ask them to keep teasing until you reply naturally to all the teases, using simple, comfortable retorts.

- *Look for 'the pop'*: Although you need to practise a variety of retorts, when you are ready, you might actually say something quite different. Children say it just 'pops out' of their mouth.

- *Be gutsy*: I practise safe retorts with children and their parents. But children often do things that adults wouldn't dare suggest. For instance, when Ben was called a 'fucking, fat faggot', he blew kisses to the bullies and jiggled his rolls of fat, and it worked! Although his action was outrageous, he did it when he was ready. You may wonder why the bully didn't whack Ben: the bully knew the game had changed and that he'd lost his power over Ben.

- *A successful retort changes your life*: Once the bully loses power, he either goes away or becomes friends. Provided you are friendly, other children will respect you now. They begin by being nice, then invite you to join their activities and want you to become their friend.

Using retorts or comebacks

Most bullying begins with words and escalates from there. The worst form of bullying is teasing. It can linger in your mind for years and affect your behaviour forever. Don't listen to the mean words, take them seriously or become upset. Instead, take the nasty bits out of the tease and return it without venom. Recycle the bully's verbal garbage by using a retort or a politically correct comeback. If you don't fight back physically or verbally, the bully has nothing to push against. He loses his physical or mental balance, starts to topple, then stops and pulls himself back to avoid being embarrassed.

A good retort boomerangs back to the bully. If the bully laughs oddly, grimaces or looks stuck for words, he is embarrassed. You have blocked his attack (see also the 'Handpower' exercise). Your power to embarrass the bully is the sting.

This is verbal martial arts. All of the following retorts have been created by children and have worked! Even traumatised children and parents can find something suitable. I have included lots of examples to defuse your pain with humour and block the bully. You can 'mix 'n' match' retorts. As long as it is assertive, not passive or aggressive, the results are great.

What's best?

- If you are shy, scared or verbally weak, use simple, easy, quick responses such as, 'Thanks for the feedback', 'And I like ice cream', 'Life's a bitch', 'And...?' or 'Pardon?'

- You might enjoy a long reply, e.g. 'I don't want to be called that name any more. Here are some new words which you can use in the future; learn them by heart and I'll test you tomorrow' (then get your retorts ready).

- Find out what the bully likes. Jack's bully loves cricket, so when the bully said, 'You're an idiot', Jack replied, 'And I like cricket.' The bully was dumbstruck.

Gentle bully blockers

Although you may be feeling frustrated, it is wise to begin with a gentle approach to block the bully. This is particularly useful if he doesn't realise what you are saying and may want to befriend you later on.

BE POSITIVE

'That was interesting. You said that twice today, and if you come back tomorrow, I'll let you say it twice again.'

'You have a different way of viewing things.'
'Have you thought about wording that differently?'
'I can see your point of view but...'

RE-LABEL OR RE-FRAME: TURN THE TEASE INTO SOMETHING POSITIVE

Bully: 'Hey stupid…'
Reply: 'Well, I didn't have Vegemite™ for breakfast.'

Bully: 'Why can't you do anything right?'
Reply: 'At least I'm still breathing.'

Bully: 'I know something you don't know.'
Reply: 'Well use that in your curriculum vitae.'

Bully: 'Your parents are so old-fashioned, they won't let you do anything.'
Reply: 'They are being caring and responsible.'

NEGOTIATE

Bully: 'Go away…'
Reply: 'If you stop annoying me I won't report you.'

Bully: 'Gossip, gossip…'
Reply: 'Do you have a gossip licence?'

Bully: 'Hey you big fart…'
Reply: 'As I don't like being bullied, can we discuss my options?'

AGREE AND ACKNOWLEDGE

Bully: 'You are so pathetic.'
Reply: 'You're so right.'

Bully: 'You've got rocks in your head.'
Reply: 'Well, I can't afford diamonds yet.'

BE THANKFUL: YOU CAN LEARN A LOT FROM BULLIES ABOUT WHO THEY ARE AND WHO YOU ARE

Bully: 'You can't play ball.'
Reply: 'Thanks for the feedback.'

Bully:	'You're an arsehole.'
Reply:	'Thanks for sharing that with me.'

Bully:	'You're a real fucking bastard.'
Reply:	'Thanks for training me in how to deal with bullies.'

BAFFLE, BLOCK AND FLUFF

Bully:	'Oh shut up.'
Reply:	'Why don't you eat a hamburger and French fries?'

Bully:	'You're such a teacher's pet.'
Reply:	'Kids love pets.'

Bully:	'Well, I'm not your friend any more!'
Reply:	'And I'm not your football any more.'

Bully:	'You are such an idiot.'
Reply:	'And I like ice cream.'

Bully:	'You don't have any friends.'
Reply:	'Yeah, I've got the personality of a used bus ticket.'

QUESTION OR CLARIFY

Bully:	'You're a lesbian.'
Reply:	'Where's your evidence?'

Bully:	'You're such a bitch.'
Reply:	'Shall I go back to my kennel now or later?'

Bully:	'You're a shit.'
Reply:	'Do you want to see the rest of my blemishes? It won't take long.' (show any warts, scars, spots, etc.)

INTELLECTUALISE OR EXPLAIN

Bully:	'You're a dumb bum.'
Reply:	'No, my brain's in my head, not my bum, so my bum can't be dumb. Maybe you meant "numb" and mixed up an "n" with a "d".' Or, 'That's politically incorrect, I'm "verbally impaired and aesthetically challenged".'

Bully: 'You're an arsehole.'
Reply: 'Explain that to me, I'm only a layperson.'

Tough bully blockers

Some children are slow learners. They need to be told they are being mean or to learn from this type of retort that they are doing the wrong thing.

BE TRUTHFUL: IT TAKES PEOPLE BY SURPRISE
Bully: 'Shut up...'
Reply: 'I think you are a real bully.'

Bully: 'Hey germ...'
Reply: 'Do you feel good when you bully me?'

CHALLENGE
Bully: 'You stutter like a broken record.'
Reply: 'I bet you can't copy me exactly!'

Bully: 'You smell.'
Reply: 'Say that again and I'll take my socks off and you can really enjoy them.'

Bully: 'You can't play with us.'
Reply: 'But competition is healthy.'

CONFRONT
Bully: 'Piss off...'
Reply: 'Who gave you permission to violate my rights?'

Bully: 'Go away, slut...'
Reply: 'If you harass me again I'll contact the school, the police, the media and a lawyer.'

Bully: 'Hey, move over...'
Reply: 'If you keep knocking me in the corridor I'll hug you back.'

DISAGREE

Bully:	'Fuck off.'
Reply:	'Dad said I'm too young.'

Bully:	'You are an idiot.'
Reply:	'Rubbish, I'm an imbecile.'

Bully:	'You are a freckle face.'
Reply:	'I'm not a freckle face, I am a speckle face.'

Bully:	'Carrot top.'
Reply:	'No, it's green and my hair is red.'

Bully:	'You're a girl.'
Reply:	'No, that was in a past life.'

EXAGGERATE: CONTRADICT AND SURPRISE

Bully:	'You're fat.'
Reply:	'Don't be ridiculous – I am enormous.'

Bully:	'You're hopeless.'
Reply:	'No, I am absolutely pathetic.'

Bully:	'You dress like a slob.'
Reply:	'No, I dress worse than an Egyptian mummy.'

FIND AN AUDIENCE NEAR OTHER CHILDREN OR TEACHERS

Bully:	'You're such a dickhead.'
Reply:	'I've got wax in my ears today – can you say that a bit louder?'

Bully's repeat (a little louder):	'You're such a dickhead.'
Reply:	'It's better but I still can't hear very well. Say that louder.'

Bully's second repeat (louder again):	'You're such a dickhead.'
Reply:	'Make it louder.'…and keep going until the bully is shouting and a teacher hears!

Various other bully blockers

It is useful to collect a bunch of simple, generic replies of different styles: a variety of retorts that work for a variety of teases. Learn them so they can 'pop out' automatically when necessary.

AUTOMATIC

'Outrageous', 'Wow', 'I hear what you say', 'Whoopee', 'Beg your pardon?', 'Really', 'Fancy that', 'Gee whiz', 'Define that for me', 'I didn't realise that', 'Sorry about that'.

CONTINUE THE GAME

Bully: 'You smell.'

Reply: 'My special smell has taken years to perfect.'

Bully
continues: 'But it's not perfect.'

Reply: 'I know, sometimes I don't get the mixture just right.'

Bully: 'You're such a nerd.'

Reply: 'I'm always like this in the morning.'

Bully
continues: 'You're like that in the afternoon.'

Reply: 'You are so observant, have you considered a career in journalism?'

FIND OPTIONS

Bully: 'You are so fat.'

Reply options: 'No, I'm just well-padded.'
'It's genetic.'
'I love to eat.'
'I'm a chocoholic.'

Bully: 'Gee, you are ugly.'

Reply options: 'No, I am cosmetically challenged.'
'I'm an ugly duckling today and one day I'll be a swan.'

'Wear some rose-coloured glasses and I'll look better.'
'I'm saving for a complete makeover.'

Bully: 'You are such a nerd/geek/wuss/dag.'

Reply options: 'No, I'm still in training.'
'I'll soon have my licence.'
'So I'm doing it properly?'
'Will I become rich and famous like Bill Gates?'

Bully: 'You're a dickhead.'

Reply options: 'Last week, I was a complete fool.'
'Is it better to be a dickhead or an arsehole?'
'When you call me a dickhead, which part of my head is the dick?'
'Two heads are better than one.'
'I'd love a photo.'

Bully: 'You're such a square.'

Reply options: 'I'm actually a circle in disguise.'
'Don't be jealous.'

Bully: 'Shorty.'

Reply options: 'I know, it's genetic.'
'There are more successful short people in the world than tall ones. I've got a greater chance of being successful if I'm small.'

Bully: 'You're gay/homo…'

Reply options: 'Explain that, I'm just a kid.'
'Don't tell my girlfriend.'
'No, I was gay yesterday! Today I'm glad and tomorrow I'll feel good, and by the weekend I'll feel great.'

Bully: 'Your mother is a tart.'

Reply options: 'Is she a jam tart or a cheese tart?'
'I hope your mother enjoys her life as much as mine does.'

Bully: 'You're an idiot.'

Reply options:	'According to psychologists, an idiot has a very low IQ, which means that I couldn't qualify for this class.' 'You said the same thing last week and the week before and I'm getting bored, it's about time you said something else.' 'No, it's Tuesday [or whatever day]. I'm only an idiot on Sundays.'
Bully:	'You're a loner.' 'Nobody likes you.' 'You've got no friends.'
Reply options:	'I know.' 'Isn't it awful?' 'Can you help me find some?' 'Do I need some?'
Bully:	'You're a wog/Aborigine/Indian/Negro/Muslim.' etc.
Reply options:	'Gee you're observant.' 'Are you an ethnologist?' 'Do you mean my race, culture or nationality?'
Bully:	'You're a nut case.'
Reply options:	'Thanks, I knew there was something missing from my diet.' 'That's right, I love peanut butter for breakfast and lunch.'

The dumbstruck look

The moment you reply in a calm, polite, assertive manner, you will surprise the bully. She can't believe it. She expects you to be upset and react, not cool, calm and collected. So she does a very funny thing: her eyes go wide, her jaw drops and her mouth opens wider; her head goes back a little. She looks *dumbstruck*, like a deer in the headlights, like a fish that's been knocked on the head. It's the 'stunned mullet look'. Bullies, like everyone else, don't like being put in their place when they make a mistake. They feel stupid, stuck and powerless. The moment you give a good retort, the bully senses that something strange and inexplicable has happened. You weren't mean but she feels uncomfortable and odd.

The subtle sting of your retort confuses the bully and she feels embarrassed. She doesn't understand that she's lost the power to hurt you. But the fear of being embarrassed again, especially in front of her mates, stops her bullying you. She gives up. Even if you don't see the dumbstruck look, you know it's worked because you feel safe – nobody bullies you. You might even smile when you tell your parents what happened!

'Handpower' exercise

Parents and kids activity

Some children are so traumatised by the bullying that they can't imagine the impact of a successful retort or other assertive behaviours. To help them, play this simple game.

1. Ask your child to sit down opposite you, on a chair of matching height. Put up your hands, ask her to do the same, and say, 'Push my hands as hard as you can'. Make sure that your hands stay upright while you are pushing. Ask your child how hard she is pushing on a scale of one to ten, and share your score, e.g. 'If you are pushing a six out of ten, then I'm pushing an eight out of ten.' Compliment her on how hard it was for you to push and how easy it was for her. Then say, 'Let's take a breather.'

2. Once again ask your child to push as hard as before, using the same 'amount' out of ten. You don't push back. Just allow your hands to stand upright but relax and flop where they are pushed. What happens?

3. Your child begins to fall over, then stops, straightens her posture, pulls back and looks confused. She wonders what's happened.

4. Ask your child, 'Why did you stop pushing?' She will say, 'Your hands went floppy' or 'You didn't push back'.

5. Then say, 'This is not good enough, I asked you to push me and you should be able to do that regardless of what I am doing. You did it before so you can do it again.' She looks confused. Then ask, 'Who took your power away?'

6. If she has difficulty understanding the underlying concept or if she looks confused, explain it by saying, 'I gave you the power to push me. When I stopped pushing, you lost your power to push me. *I took your power away.* If you had pushed harder, then you would have lost your balance and fallen on top of me. Falling on a parent is not a big deal, but if I were someone else, you would have felt embarrassed if you had fallen into my lap. Nobody likes to feel embarrassed, including bullies. When the bully has the "dumbstruck look" it means she won't repeat anything that embarrasses her in front of her mates. So if you respond correctly, the bully must stop.'

7. Although the 'dumbstruck look' can seem very funny to a child who has been bullied for a long time, say, 'When we played this game I didn't laugh, even though I knew what would happen. You must promise not to laugh in front of the bully if she looks dumbstruck, as that would give away our secret. You can do so later on.' (This helps her visualise her future success.)

8. Then say, 'It doesn't matter whether people bully you physically or verbally, you can give away your power or keep it for yourself.'

Responding to bullying

This section includes a variety of examples from my work with students. Some were used to de-sensitise, to create humour and as a visualisation exercise. Others empowered the child by providing possible options. The best way to respond will depend upon what is appropriate at your school, the school's actions to stop the bullying, and the number of bullies. Ask your parent(s) about this.

- *Be prepared*: Use good eye contact, a neutral face and calm body language. Remain calm: if you become angry and attack, the situation will get out of control.

- *Learn martial arts*: These programmes are effective for both targets and bullies. They train shy and vulnerable children to move assertively, coach children to protect themselves by defusing rather than aggravating stressful encounters, and train bullies to control their behaviours. If necessary, children can fight back skilfully when threatened.

- *Record it*: Use a notebook in front of the bully to record any bullying behaviours. You can clarify, e.g. 'Did you raise your right eyebrow and shrug your right shoulder when you called me an idiot?' Then work out who to tell, e.g. your teacher, the principal, the bully's parents, or other children. Bullies don't like evidence and publicity – nobody is proud of being a bully. Of course, it probably won't be long before kids use phones with cameras to photograph or video bullies (without permission). Show the bully you are collecting evidence.

- *Create confidence boosters*: Find security objects to take to school that boost your confidence, e.g. an alarm bracelet, a whistle, a real or toy mobile phone, headphones, or chew gum.

- *Protect yourself*: Carry an inflatable rubber baseball bat, cushion, raincoat or overcoat to protect yourself. It would certainly get attention and a laugh.

- *Get fit*: Many targets look weak and wimpy. Don't spend your free time in a library or hidden inside a computer. You need to play outdoors, exercise, go to the gym, play sport or dance. Even walking for 20 minutes five times a week makes a difference. Then you can gesticulate, duck, run quickly or protect yourself physically.

- *Learn eye movements*: Learn how to roll your eyes, move them up or down, from side to side, or just practise staring into space. You can confuse the bully.

- *Be loud*: You probably have a loud voice at home, so do the same at school. Use it with the bully in class, in the yard or on public transport. Make sure that everyone looks around, stares at the bully and embarrasses him.

- *Scream*: Practise screaming loudly, so that everyone recognises an assault. I saw one girl who sat paralysed while a boy felt up between her legs in class. If a girl is touched on the breast or any other private part of her body, she should speak firmly or shout loudly, 'I want you to stop doing that to me.' She can blow a whistle, use a personal alarm, pinch or punch back, or get up and move away, even in class. Similarly, boys can do the same if sexually harassed.

- *Do nothing*: When a girl attacked my niece in the street, my niece realised that if she hit back, the fight would escalate. While she was doing nothing, her friends intervened and stopped it. Sometimes we make it worse when we fight back.

- *Attack back*: In an emergency, you need to fight back because nothing else has worked. If you are prepared to take this dangerous course of action, ask your parents to help you plan your defence, build your resources and limit your attack.

How to block nonverbal bullying

There are many types of bullying apart from teasing. These include harassment, cyber bullying, exclusion and physical bullying. Here are some examples of ways to deal with them (and remember to check with your parents first).

VIA EMAILS, CHAT GROUPS AND TEXT MESSAGES

- Don't reply to nasty comments.

- Change your code/password, and inform only close friends.

- Alter your voicemail so that the bully doesn't know who he is calling.

- Inform your parents and get them to reply.

- Block the bully's server/email address.

- Tape-record or print out a copy and give it to the school, your parents, or the police – it may be a criminal offence.

- Reply: 'Your message has been forwarded to the crime squad'.

- Turn off your phone.

PUSHING, SHOVING, BUMPING, HAIR-PULLING

- Say, 'Don't come close to me because my socks are smelly' or 'I farted.'

- Tickle him: no-one gets into trouble for tickling at school, and bullies won't like it. If the bully pulls your hair, simultaneously tickle him under the arm.

- Be clumsy: allow your books to fall over the bully and make a fuss over apologising.

- Make a squeaky noise: squeeze a rubber duck when the bully bumps you. The noise creates fun, attention and may change the bully's game.

BOOKS OR POSSESSIONS REMOVED FROM DESK OR LOCKER, OR PUSHED OVER, BROKEN OR HIDDEN

- Don't bring your mobile phone and other valuables to school, or leave them at the school's office.

- Report the damage: bullies who do bad things risk trouble.

- Put up signs: advertise bully behaviours near the staffroom, in the classroom, library, computer room, corridor, playground, bus shelter and train station.

- Petition: ask children who don't like the bully's behaviour to sign a petition. They can use an imaginary name if they are scared, e.g. 'Spoodle wants Bulldog to stop...'.

- Charge them: give them a bill for the cost of the goods that have been damaged or stolen, and send a copy to their parents. Include a warning that if it is not paid within seven days, you will go to the principal or the police.

FLICKING WATER, PAPER BALLS, RUBBER BANDS, ETC.

- Water throwers: put up your brightest or largest umbrella and smile as you walk past, or wear a hat in class. With your parents' permission, empty a glass of water in the bully's locker or on their desk and say, 'I was told to return what doesn't belong to me.'

- Place all the rubber bands or bits of paper in a glass jar on your desk. Label it, 'Bully darts'.

- Paper flickers: stuff a huge pile of newspaper in their locker or place a few rolls of toilet paper on their desk so they don't need to get their ammunition from the toilets.

EXCLUSION, ISOLATION FROM THE SOCIAL GROUP (SEE ALSO CHAPTER 13)

- Make sure you are friendly, blend in and have fun.

- Suck up to the leader, e.g. ask about his weekends, hobbies.

- If you are suddenly isolated by the group, contact each child individually at home and say, 'I am feeling very hurt. What have I done to make you exclude me?' They may snigger but deep down they know how you feel because everybody has been excluded at times. If they don't care, you know they're not real friends.

- Ask your teachers for help. They can organise a role-play about the impact of exclusion on students.

- Find other friends, even if they are less popular.

- Move things around in his desk or locker. When he complains, say, 'It can't be me because according to you I don't exist.'

- Behave like a statue right next to him. Then eat some popular food without offering him any.

- Leave a school controlled by 'bitches' or 'bulldogs'.

WHISPERING, GIGGLING, LAUGHING, WRITING NOTES ABOUT YOU

- Say, 'If you do mean things behind my back, then you don't care about me.'

- Say, 'I don't like you whispering behind my back. If you have the guts, tell me to my face; if not, then stop.'

- Take a bow – you have obviously entertained them.

- Take any notes, emails, tapes of phone conversations, etc. to the teacher.

POINTING, STARING, MIMICKING YOUR VOICE OR MANNER

- Say, 'I can't see the corners of your mouth when you giggle as I walk past. Can you do it in front of me next time?'

- Ask, 'What else could you do to have fun without bullying me?'

- Mirror his behaviour and copy exactly what he does. Even better, ask your friends to copy you and do it all together.

- When the bully displays nasty nonverbal gestures with his eyes, eyebrows, lips, shoulders, fingers, etc., identify this part of his body, look concerned, make eye contact and ask, 'What's wrong with your eyebrows?'

- Inform the bully, 'I belong to the actors' union. I can't entertain you for free. You owe me $10.' Send a bill to his parents for 'Bully Entertainment'.

- If you don't wear a school uniform, wear a badge or a T-shirt painted with a message like, 'Bullies are kid destroyers'.

NOT SHARING SEATS, TURNING HIS BACK, TAKING AWAY YOUR CHAIR AS YOU SIT DOWN

- If he won't share a seat, try to sit on his lap.

- The bully says, 'This seat is saved.' Reply options: 'I don't feel like moving today', 'Where's your ticket?', 'Was it lost before?', 'I'll look after it carefully', 'I know, but my father said I could sit here.'

- Say in a clear, loud voice in front of an audience or a teacher, 'I'm very angry at your mean behaviour' to embarrass the bully or force the teacher to act.

Kids activity

Write down the list of bully blockers you can use:

Teases:..

Physical:..

Social exclusion:...

Cyber:...

Any other:..

Key points – your power tools

- Strip the tease.
- Consider all options.
- Use effective communication skills.
- Have regular target practice.
- Use humour.
- Be natural/genuine/cool.
- Don't react, retaliate or be a 'smart-arse'.
- Allow it to 'pop out'.

What to do
- Use your power tools.

13

Develop a support network – Secret 6

Jackie is an only child who doesn't know how to relate to friendly kids or deal with kids who are mean. She becomes nasty when upset. The rest of her class regard her as babyish and overprotected. She is intelligent and gets good marks in class, but it's hard for the other kids to like or respect her. Nobody wants to work with her doing projects because she wants to do it her way. She gets upset when kids make silly comments or banter. She doesn't like fooling around, so they can't have fun working with her. Once she began a project with a group of girls, but they decided to do something else and left her. She had to do it on her own. It was hard but she persisted. Unfortunately, the other kids received a better mark because they had pooled all their resources. She was upset and could not understand why she hadn't done as well as the group.

Social beings survive better

Clearly, life has its ups and downs. Adults who cope best with the stresses and traumas of life generally have caring, supportive networks. Children with good social skills have more fun, share their problems, work out solutions and obtain group support for their activities and actions. When you belong to a number of groups, you obtain the self-esteem and emotional support you need to cope during stressful times. You aren't alone. Instead of being limited by your own resources, you utilise the support, feedback, information and skills from others to improve. You regard feedback as constructive, because generally it is well intentioned and well informed. Then you make the appropriate changes. Thus, you achieve more because others help you with their contacts, knowledge and experience.

When you belong to a tribe, whether it is a sports team, a drama club or the neighbourhood gang, you feel more secure, accepted and respected. When you have friends, you are happier at school, despite any learning difficulties, physical problems or family stresses, compared to children with a small, insecure or unstable network of friends.

Children who have a solid group of friends are generally less likely to be bullied than the loner or the child with a single friend. That's because most bullies are wimps who avoid children with a strong network of assertive friends.

Sharon was bullied for years at her old school. Eventually she moved on to a nice, new school. Everyone was friendly. One little girl wanted Sharon to be her best friend. 'What should I do?' Sharon asked me. I replied, 'No-one lives on rice alone. You also eat potato, pasta, chocolate, chips and ice cream. You need a bunch of good friends rather than being handcuffed to one friend. Then you can improve your social skills, widen your network and block bullies. If you lost one friend for any reason, e.g. they moved far away, you still have others. You won't be scared about being assertive because if friends don't like you being yourself, then you can make some more because you have the skills.'

The social skills formula

Below are the core elements in developing effective social skills and friendships. They include some important points from the first five secrets.

1. Be friendly and chat to lots of children

Use good eye contact, have a relaxed face (not a 'lemon-juice' face), and smile regularly to show that you are not shy, arrogant or mean. Chat about everyday stuff as though you were meeting on holidays. Your manner is more important than your words. Chat can lead to trust.

2. Show real interest in other children

Don't worry about how you feel and appear – that makes you a belly-button watcher. Imagine you are standing at one end of a very thin, high bridge. Don't look down and stress out. Focus upon walking over the bridge towards the other kid. Ask questions that show interest in what she is doing, and what you can do together. The more genuine interest you give to other children, the more they will give to you. Show special interest in at least five children.

3. Give empathy

When you see someone giving a juicy bone to a dog, you feel pleased for the dog. This is called empathy. Empathy means that we understand some of what another being is feeling. You are not the dog getting the bone, so you don't know *exactly* what the dog feels. Similarly, you don't really know what another child is experiencing, but you can show care and concern by sharing in her experience – whether it is fun, fear or frustration.

4. Be yourself

Most children feel uncomfortable with someone who is always 'nice'. It's hard to respect and trust someone you don't know, and this happens when kids wear a 'nice' mask. Children need to know what you really think, feel and want before they will trust you. Then they can work out how to relate to you. So use the 'I' word and express yourself clearly. It is up to them how they respond.

5. Negotiate differences

Whenever people relate, there will be differences of opinion, just like at home. It's normal to share your opinions by discussing, confronting and negotiating differences. Sometimes you win, sometimes the other kid will win, at other times you both compromise. If you can't create a win-win relationship with your current friends, find friends who listen, share and resolve differences together. Avoid those who try to denigrate or control you.

6. Real friends are committed to one another

There is a difference between real friends and casual friends. Casual friends come and go, whereas true friends really care about you. They show their commitment by maintaining regular contact, e.g. spending lunchtimes together, after-school visits, sleepovers. They invest in their friendship and don't expect more than they give. They mend their disappointments and have reasonable expectations. They don't take one another for granted but give each other space because they're not padlocked together. They forgive, forget and move on. Are you and your friends committed to your friendship? Although children banter and muck around, your friends may bully you or may not protect you when someone is bullying you.

If they don't respect your feelings when you tell them how you feel, using the 'I' word, then they are not a true friend. Then it's better to find friends who can respect and help you.

7. Just do it

Popular children are always making social arrangements. They build a social life by working at it. The more often you contact kids to make arrangements, the more social you become. Don't hang around the computer or library at lunchtime. Spending time with the same kids most lunchtimes develops your regular support group. Inviting children home regularly means that you can get to know one another better.

8. Use all your feedback

Feedback is a fantastic tool. If you say or do something that another child doesn't like, she will show you immediately by a look, word or action. Find out why she reacted in this way. Was she pleased or upset by your behaviour? She will show you very quickly if she can discuss and share feedback, or she'll disappear from your social life. Don't worry: if you tried your best to be open, you'll find someone else to play with who is more flexible and understanding.

9. Nobody is perfect

You are not always the best-behaved, most conscientious kid. Often you just think and talk about yourself. So do your friends. Everyone makes mistakes. Friends may be inconsiderate, difficult or mean, and you may not always know why they behave the way they do. You can't judge them until you understand their experiences. Don't expect friends to be perfect; be happy if they are a good friend 75+ percent of the time.

10. Collect a variety of friends

Although it's really important to have a bunch of friends your own age, it's also good to have other friends. They can be your age, older or younger. You can make them at school, at sporting activities outside school, in your neighbourhood, at dance, drama or martial-arts classes, in religious organisations, Scouts or at holiday camps. Just like your parents, you can make friends in a variety of places who will extend your social life, make you more interesting and support you when your schoolmates are being difficult.

I like reading holiday brochures, but I would prefer to go there. Similarly, be wary of friends you 'meet' inside a computer. They may be nice, but they aren't real friends until you make a real, live connection.

The list of tips in the following box has helped many children have a better social life.

Developing your child's social skills

Parents activity

- Encourage your child to play with other children at school, home and locally.

- Practise chatting at home at meal times, without any electronic 'blah blah'.

- Limit electronic time, which interferes with socialising time.

- Arrange 'get-togethers' with extended family and friends.

- Organise outings where she can socialise with others her own age. This helps create friendships anywhere and builds social confidence.

- She may need help in picking up the phone and making social arrangements. You could say, 'I'll give you until Thursday and then I will ring myself.'

- Invite children over and show your child how to make guests feel welcome.

- Give your child a game or activity to attract other children at lunchtime.

- Point out when she relates positively to others e.g. 'You can smile, show interest and have fun with your cousins – just do the same at school.'

- Enrol your child in a social skills, assertiveness training or communications skills workshop.

Types of relationship

There are three types of relationship:

Parents activity

1. passive – the child has little power and tags along

2. aggressive – the child becomes bossy and bullies, and

3. assertive – power is shared equally by negotiation.

- Encourage your child to have assertive friends, who protect her. This will enhance your child's self-esteem so she will be less likely to be bullied.

- Some adults believe they are helping a child by allowing some friends and eliminating others. Children play with kids who reflect the way they see themselves. If she chooses an 'unusual' child, this reveals her self-image. Be careful with eliminating unusual children: there may be nobody else for that child to play with. As long as these kids don't cause trouble, it's a start. Your child will become more selective once her social skills improve.

- Suggest some spring-cleaning. Show your child how to get rid of friends who are bullying her, even if these children are popular.

How does your child score socially?

Parents activity

Children's social needs vary and grow as they mature. You can fill out this social score sheet. Then ask your child's teacher to compare it to the peer group. The teacher may know if your child is socially competent or requires improvement. Some teachers may use a sociogram (or friendship chart) to illustrate your child's social standing in class. Then help your child improve her social score.

Social score sheet

Social involvement	Never	Occasionally	Weekly	Regularly
Uses the phone/Internet for a chat (with real friends)				
Uses the phone to make arrangements				
Uses the phone/Internet to do homework with friends				
Socialises with the same friends at lunchtime				
Mentions the same names regularly at the dinner table				
Expresses concern about classmates who are stressed				
Organises social arrangements (weekends, holidays)				
Invites friends her own age for activities, e.g. sleepovers				
Participates in sporting or other activities with peer group				
Receives birthday invitations				
Shows pleasure and interest in meeting friends				
Buys or takes gifts to other children				
Relates with ease to strangers				

Kids activity

Identifying potential new friends

Here is an exercise to help you build a core group of friends and a social support network. There are probably some friendly children in your class. Write down the names of children who:

- share ideas or things and cooperate with you in games or on projects:

I. .... 2. .... 3. ....

- are fair, give and take, share power:

I. .... 2. .... 3. ....

- care, show interest and empathy with others:

I. .... 2. .... 3. ....

- are fun and enjoy doing the things you enjoy:

I. .... 2. .... 3. ....

- say or show that they like you:

I. .... 2. .... 3. ....

- you like (you show this by what you say or do):

I. .... 2. .... 3. ....

- are or who do something you like:

I. .... 2. .... 3. ....

If you write down some names more frequently than others, they could become a friend. You know what the next step is! Be real, show interest and make arrangements.

Your friendship groups

No-one has lots of real friends. Most kids have a core of true, close friends with whom they share their ups and downs. Then they have a group of acquaintances with whom they socialise. They are not as close to them emotionally and don't share everything to the extent they do with their core group. But both groups change constantly, depending upon what is going on in your life and theirs.

You need a good, sympathetic group of children to play with at school. There are three main social groups at school: the popular, the middle and the 'nerdy' groups. Try to become friendly with the middle group: there is less threat if you are different, it is safer socially, and they are more likely to help you deal with bullies.

The friendship game

You need a strong network of decent friends your own age at school to develop social skills, block bullies or stop you bullying others.

- Become closer to three to five classmates – it will take a few weeks.

- Belonging to a group, even if they are unpopular, is better than being padlocked to a best friend. Also, teachers are more likely to believe a group of witnesses than one friend.

- Make social arrangements – visit friends, cousins or neighbours.

- Make your friends welcome when they visit your home.

- Make sure your friends take turns in sharing games, etc.

- What else can you do?

Kids activity

Your support network

Identify all those people who can help you when you need it:

- parents, aunts/uncles, grandparents

- brothers, sisters, cousins

- neighbours, doctor, sports coach, Scout leader, drama teacher

- students, e.g. close friends, casual friends, friendly kids in class

- peer-group mediator, older students, school captain, etc.

- teachers, principal, year coordinator

- school counsellor, school psychologist, school nurse, welfare officer, school minister

- chat groups, bullying websites, telephone helplines, and

- the media, the police, your local member of parliament, the mayor.

This is a mind map. Fill in the names of your support network.

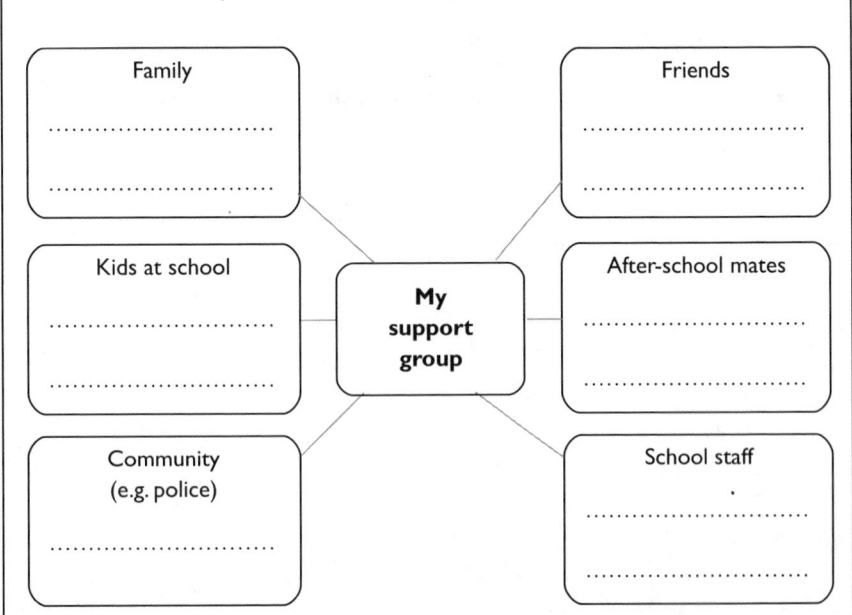

Help your child avoid hot spots

Parents activity

Although some children are bullied in class only, your child may be bullied in other parts of the school. Write down where the bullying occurs, e.g. on the way to or from school, in the playground, in the corridors, at the lockers, near the canteen, etc. Then write down how your child can protect himself, e.g. walk with a friend, stay near the staffroom at recess, avoid lockers when bullies are there, and so on.

Key points

- Children who belong to a social tribe cope better than those who are alone.
- Children need social skills to improve their support networks.
- Adults can help children develop support networks.

What to do

- Take action to become more social and make good friends.
- Work out safe routes to and from school.
- Who is part of your support network?

Teachers' supplement

Issues for teachers

How can you tell if it's bullying and not just shared fun?

Sometimes it can be difficult to differentiate between a bullying incident and a bit of friendly banter. Teachers' and students' perceptions of such an incident can depend on the type of interaction, the location, the responses of witnesses, the grapevine effect, whether those interacting are 'friends', the frequency of such interaction, and its impact on the target. Sometimes a target claims he is having fun because he is scared to complain and exacerbate the bullying. Remember, bullying can be physical, verbal (teasing), anti-social (excluding) or electronic in nature. And where there is bullying, there is always damage. Obtain the story from everyone involved. Aim for reconciliation, not evidence of wrongdoing.

See Chapter 1, 'Types of bullying' (pp. 17–21) and 'Non-bullying interaction' (pp. 25–26).

How can you tell if someone is a bully or a target?

Bullying is a game. The players can sometimes change sides, making it difficult to distinguish between target and bully. They are affected by the onlookers and by the school's interventions (or lack of them). A malicious bully has no empathy for his target, enjoying the distress; whereas a non-malicious bully often appears oblivious to the target's distress. Targets can be vulnerable, provocative, or just in the wrong place at the wrong time.

See all of Chapter 2.

What do you do if there is a bully in your class?

The key issue is to realise that the bully has been trained at home, and his behaviours have been reinforced at school. Thus you need to obtain his version of events, treat him with respect and understanding, and coach him in appropriate social skills. Then reinforce appropriate behaviours and provide consequences for inappropriate behaviours (e.g. involve his parents). Alternatively, use class feedback on conflict resolution approaches to help him modify his behaviours.

See Chapter 7, 'Strategies to reduce school bullying' (pp.110–25), and all of Chapter 9.

How can you help a target in your class?

There are many factors that make a target more vulnerable to bullying than his peers, including his family structure and accompanying stresses, social difficulties and personality. Make sure you obtain his version of the bullying incident(s), provide empathy and understanding, and help him develop bully-blocking skills. You should involve his parents if the bullying continues, and refer him for counselling if it does not improve. Encourage all students to oppose bullying, and try to find a caring bunch of children to support the target.

See all of Chapter 5, especially the exercises on pp.69–73('If I gave you a million dollars', 'Take a chance', 'What are three things you can do to feel powerful?'); all of Chapter 11 (especially the exercises); and Chapter 12, 'Using retorts or comebacks' (pp.206–14), and the 'Handpower' exercise (pp.215–16).

What role does the school play in allowing or discouraging bullying?

See Chapter 3, 'The role of the school' (pp.38–40), and all of Chapter 7.

How can you reduce bullying at your school?

See all of Chapter 7.

How can you best deal with parents of bullies and targets?

See Chapter 6, 'Dealing with your child's school' (pp.98–107), and Chapter 7, Point 6, 'Train students, staff and parents' (pp.114–18).

Class topics

Why is bullying bad?

Students can discuss the harm caused by bullying, focusing upon the physical, psychological, academic, social and self-esteem damage.

See all of Chapter 4.

Why do some kids bully?

There are many reasons why children bully. Some are copying role models learnt at home or school, others are feeling hurt, rejected or insecure. Some are propelled by a primitive survival instinct that leads them to join the mob and attack the vulnerable person.

See all of Chapter 3, especially 'The core issues' (pp.44–45).

How can you help kids understand the bullying 'game'?

See Chapter 1, 'The bullying game' (pp.21–26), and all of Chapter 9.
Provide role-plays of different types of bullying and then discuss.

How can all kids protect themselves from bullying?

The child who has a bunch of good friends and is generally friendly and caring to others is highly unlikely to be bullied. If a child is bullied, he or she should disguise their anger or fear and respond in a neutral manner – like confronting an animal. Targets of bullying must not show their distress. If the bullying is bad, they must get help from adults. When adults are slow to protect them, including parents, the targets must continue reminding them until the target(s) feel safe.

See Chapter 8, 'The feelings formula' (pp.137–46); Chapter 10, 'The three essential steps to good self-esteem (pp.168–79– includes lots of exercises); and all of Chapter 13.

How effective are rehearsed retorts to bullying if they are taught in class and the bullies know what will happen?

Children know the game in tennis, football or debating, but this does not detract from the fun involved or the skills required. Set the ground rules, e.g. let the retort just 'pop out', be generic, be very original, etc. Get kids to coach each other on the best way to use retorts. Rehearsing retorts in class allows the kids to learn the correct, assertive, non-aggressive way to use them.

See Chapter 12.

What can kids do if they see bullying happening? How can they best deal with physical, verbal, anti-social or electronic bullying?

Bullies are not stupid. They want to be accepted by their peers. Thus the peer group or the onlookers play a powerful role in condoning or enabling bullying. Teachers should teach students what to say and how to intervene when they witness bullying. They must give students the power to report an incident, anonymously or publicly, without fear of being labelled or risking attack themselves. And, if necessary, teachers should discipline a whole group who allow bullying to continue.

Be prepared: bullying can occur anywhere. Regardless of whether kids mean to hurt or not, we need options for dealing with each type of bullying. Discuss with the students what they would do and work out what is best.

See Chapter 3, 'The role of the school' (pp.38–39); Chapter 7, Point 3, 'Investigate the bullying' (pp.112–13), and 'Methods for managing bullying incidents' (pp.120–21); and all of Chapter 12, especially 'Responding to bullying' (pp.216–22).

Where else does bullying occur?

Sadly, schools are not the only havens for bullying. Bullying can occur at home, at work or elsewhere. Students may like to consider and compare the often inhumane treatment of Indigenous people, older people, homosexuals, women and children in the light of bullying and its abuse of power.

Author's notes

Page 16 '**About one in five students is bullied regularly, and around one in five bully regularly.**': Assoc. Prof. Ken Rigby, in a lecture, 2005.

Page 22 '**Research has shown that some pick on nearly everyone at the beginning of a year, until someone reacts.**': Hara Estroff Marano, 'Big. Bad. Bully' in *Psychology Today*, 28, 5, Sept./Oct. 1995. She quotes Dr Gary Ladd, Professor of Psychology at the University of Illinois, who believes that bullies use a 'shopping process' to find their victims.

Page 23 '**Dr Debra Pepler has found an ongoing relationship between the bully and the target.**': This section is based on the work of Toronto psychologist Dr Debra Pepler, whose work is cited in Estroff Marano, 'Big. Bad. Bully', *Psychology Today*, 28, 5, Sept./Oct. 1995. She video-recorded children in the playground to demonstrate the bully–victim 'dance'.

Page 29 '**...the non-malicious, or "the fowl that plays foul"**': There are two types of bullies, according to Ken Rigby: the malicious and non-malicious. I call them the 'saltwater crocodiles' and the 'fowls that play foul'. See also Rigby, Ken, *Bullying in Schools and What to do About It*, ACER, Melbourne, 1996.

Page 35 **Shy child checklist**: This list is based on what children and their parents have told me. Parents often say that it describes their child perfectly.

Page 38 '**Most kids are affected by *where* they are, not who they are.**': Based on the comment, 'Clearly, nice ordinary people are affected by where they are, not who they are', in an article by Ian Parkin in *The Age* referring to Professor Philip Zimbardo's work. See also Zimbardo, *APA Monitor*, October, 2004; Robert M. Sapolsky, *A Primate's Memoir: A Neuroscientist's Unconventional Life Among the Baboons*, Scribner, New York, 2002; and the 'obedience experiments' of Stanley Milgram at Yale.

Page 38 '**Pat Ferris has applied this concept to workplace bullying; it also provides a handy description of how schools approach it.**': Ferris,

Patricia, 'A personal view. A preliminary typology of organisational response to allegations of workplace bullying: see no evil, hear no evil, speak no evil' in *British Journal of Guidance & Counselling*, Vol. 32, No. 3, August 2004.

Page 40 '**The research clearly shows that schools should develop a closer working relationship with parents to reduce bullying.**': See also my chapter in McGrath, H. and Noble, T. (eds), *Bullying Solutions*, Pearson, Sydney, 2005.

Page 44 '**Dan Olveus, the Norwegian anti-bullying pioneer, believes that many targets come from overprotective families.**': Targets tend to be close to their parents and may have parents who can be described as overprotective. Batsche and Knoff 1994; Olveus 1993.

Page 53 '**The body responds to extreme stress by "releasing a cascade of cortisol, adrenaline and other hormones that can damage brain cells, impair memory and set in motion a long-lasting and worsening disregulation of the body's complex biochemistry".**': Butler, Kay, 'The biology of fear', *The Family Therapy Networker*, July/August 1996. Professor Rachel Yehuda, Mt Sinai School of Medicine, New York, has also written extensively on the effects of post-traumatic stress disorder. They include decreased levels of cortisol, increased glucocortid receptor sensitivity, stronger negative feedback inhibition and hypersensitivity. Basically, this means that reduced levels of cortisol prevent adrenaline from flowing, causing the victim to remain in a powerless state.

Trauma can lead to damage in the hippocampus and can inhibit memory and learning skills.

Page 54 **Post-traumatic stress disorder**: This is a simplified version of the diagnostic category for PTSD as described by the American Psychiatric Association in *Diagnostic and Statistical Manual of Mental Disorders, 4th ed.* (DSM–IV), Washington DC, 1994.

Page 54 '**Bullying can harm targets for years after leaving school.**': Studies demonstrate that being bullied at school significantly increases the target's risk of susceptibility to anxiety disorders – such as social phobia, obsessive-compulsive disorders, schizophrenia, depression and post-traumatic stress disorder – in later life. See for example the following: Murray, Bridget, 'School phobias hold many children back', *American Psychology Association Monitor*, Sept. 1997; Gilmartin, Brian G., 'Peer Group Antecedents of Severe Love-shyness in Males', *Journal of Personality*, Duke University Press, 55, 3, Sept. 1987; Dr Margaret Gunther's pilot study at the University of New England, Armidale, January 1998; Rigby, Ken, *Bullying in Schools and What to do About It*, ACER, Melbourne, 1996; and Rigby, Ken, 'Can adverse peer relations at school drive children to suicide?' Lecture at International School of Psychology XXth Annual Colloquium, Melbourne, 1997.

Page 55 '**More people get bullied at work than at school.**': Workplace bullying occurs as readily in the elegant offices of a law firm as in the rough confines of an apprentice's shed. While the school target can exhibit social and schoolwork difficulties, the target of workplace bullying is usually a socially competent, conscientious employee. Workplace bullying occurs more frequently, has greater toxicity and creates a more devastating impact than school bullying. In addition to the personal injuries, it increases operational costs and reduces productivity. Not all school targets are bullied at work: some become bullies, while some adults experience bullying for the first time in the workplace. Counselling targets of school bullying is a brief process, whereas counselling people who are being bullied at work can take longer and, if they are too injured to work, it can take many years. The research into workplace bullying shows that more than 15 percent of employees are bullied at work and more in some industries. This is a 'guesstimate' based on a variety of studies: Prof. Heinz Leyman obtained a figure of 3.5 percent in Scandinavia (Leyman 1997), but the Workplace Bullying Project Team, Griffith University, Queensland (2001) arrived at a figure of 15 percent based on a number of British and American studies. Drs Gary and Ruth Namie in the US also quote this figure based on their own research.

Page 55 '**Most bystanders don't enjoy bullying as a spectator sport or as reality television.**': Rigby, Ken & Slee, Phillip T., 'Bullying among Australian school children: Reported behaviour and attitudes toward victims', *Journal of Social Psychology*, University of South Australia, Adelaide, 131, 5 Oct. 1991, pp. 615–27.

Page 56 '**[Bullies] may experience depression, anxiety, suicidal**

thoughts and trauma at school and later.': Bullies are often more likely to have a criminal record by the time of their mid-twenties, more likely to bash their wives and abuse their children. See Estroff Marano, Hara, 'Big. Bad. Bully', *Psychology Today*, 28, 5, Sept./Oct. 1995. Young bullies have a one-in-four chance of having a criminal record by age 30 (Huesmann, L.R., Eron, L.D., Lefkowitz, M.M. and Walder, L.O., 'Stability of aggression over time and generations', *Developmental Psychology* (20) 1120–1134, 1984). Daniel Goleman (author of *Emotional Intelligence*), writing in the *American Psychology Association Monitor*, October 1998, discussed the need for children to develop emotional intelligence. This includes being aware of their own feelings, handling distressing emotions, motivating themselves towards achievement, understanding emotions in others, and possessing basic social skills. Children who do not learn these skills are 'more likely to be the schoolyard bullies or the schoolyard rejects'.

Page 92 '**If your child is a bully**': With thanks to Kidscape, UK.

Page 108 '**Current research demonstrates that most primary schools reduce bullying by 15 percent and sceondary schools by 12 percent.**': Lecture presented at the 2005 conference on school bullying, Melbourne, organised by the National Coalition Against Bullying. Prof Ken Rigby is the major researcher on school bullying in Australia, and Dr Peter Smith is a major UK researcher.

Page 109 '**The research into workplace bullying indicates that more than 15 percent of employees are se-**

riously bullied at work…': This is a 'guesstimate' based on a variety of studies: Prof Heinz Leyman found a figure of 3.5 percent in Scandinavia (Leyman 1997), but the Workplace Bullying Project Team at Griffith University, 2004, arrived at 15 percent based on a number of British and American studies. Drs Gary and Ruth Namie also quote this figure from their research. Many studies claim that bullying can reach higher than 50 percent.

Page 109 'In an Australian study, about 50 percent of teachers were bullied – usually by colleagues, but also by parents and students.': *Newsmonth*, Vol 24, No. 7, 2004 Unionsafe Survey on Workplace Bullying, NSW Independent Teachers' Union. See also BBC News website 12/04/03: 'One out of every two teachers has been bullied at school – often by their head teachers, according to a survey.' This means that many teachers feel abused and unsafe, while others bully. Both may model inappropriate behaviours to their students. Teachers cannot be expected to support a whole-school anti-bullying policy while bullying or being bullied themselves.

Page 115 'The majority of bullying incidents are witnessed by peers. When they intervene, they are successful 50 percent of the time.': Ken Rigby, lecture for National Coalition Against Bullying, 2005.

Page 118 '7. Improve the physical environment': With thanks to Professor Donna Cross.

Page 120 'The method of shared concern.': See Pikas, A., 'The common concern method for the treatment of mobbing', E. Roland and E. Munthe (eds), *Bullying – an International Perspective*, Fulton, London, 1989. Pikas has designed this method to help students coexist rather than to establish what happened and who was to blame.

Page 121 'The no-blame approach.': See Maines and Robinson, *Crying for Help – the No-Blame Approach to Bullying*, Lucky Duck Publishing, Bristol, 1997.

Page 121 'Restorative practices.': With thanks to David Moore and Margaret Thorsborne. This conflict-resolution method, also known as restorative justice or conferencing, can be used to resolve some difficult situations at school, in the workplace, the criminal justice system and the community. It involves a formally-structured conversation between everyone involved in a dispute or an aggressive incident. This could include students, onlookers, teachers, parents and local community personnel. Some school staff need to be trained as conference facilitators. They need to determine what happened, how it has affected people, and what might now be done to improve the situation – as opposed to who has done the wrong thing and what should be done to them. Conferencing is consistent with the principles of deliberative democracy and procedural fairness. Participants are given an opportunity, in a specific sequence, to talk about what has happened, and how they have been affected. They then consider together how the situation might be improved, how specific harms might be repaired, and how the group can minimise further destructive conflict. The conference agreement is recorded in writing, signed, and a copy provided to each participant. The outcomes can vary from establishing a shared understanding of what happened, to an apology, to changing dysfunctional systems, e.g. changing lockers or occupying bored kids at recess. Then those involved can learn and move on.

The following example is to encourage schools to share their successes and to find new methods. Don't just adopt the latest trend. Teachers working at the ground level can be very creative and innovative as they find simple ideas that work with their children. Paul McBride has been developing a small, simple incident and observation booklet that teachers can use in the yard and maintain as part of the school records.

Page 122 '**Paul McBride has been developing a small, simple incident and observation booklet...**': Paul McBride is Student Wellbeing Coordinator at Holy Family Primary School, Geelong. The booklet is part of his thesis.

Page 122 '**Some time ago, Karen McDonald, a primary-school counsellor, sent me a copy of her policies and programmes.**': Karen McDonald is the counsellor at Dakota Meadows Middle School, Mankato, Minnesota, US.

Page 182 '**Most kids judge each other in the first four seconds!**': Author's personal opinion.

Acknowledgements

I am grateful to the many children, parents, teachers and schools who have given me support and feedback. They provided the core of this book. I am indebted to Mount Scopus Memorial College for the personal experience as a school target and the professional experience as a school psychologist to help targets, obtained during my 30-year association with them.

Many people and organisations have inspired, encouraged, supported and helped me while writing *Bullybusting*, the first edition of this book, and now *Bully Blocking*, this new and revised edition. They include the Australian Psychological Society, which gave me the opportunity to improve my media skills, the Australian National Association for Mental Health, the Augustine Centre, the National Coalition Against Bullying, Victims of Crime Assistance League, and the National Speakers' Association of Australia.

My thanks go to Val Besag, Christine Briggs, Brian Burdekin, Michael Carr-Gregg, Prof Donna Cross, Pam Carroll, Stale Einarsen, Pat Ferris, Ken Fisher, Morry Fraid, Andrew Fuller, Jeffrey Gerrard, Coosje Griffiths, Don Grose, Barbara Guest, Ian Jeffries, Barbara John, John King, Susan Limber, Paul McCarthy, Helen McGrath, Karen McDonald, David Moore, Sean Miller, Rod Myer, Dan Olveus, Marvin Oka, Fabiola Pantea, Judith Paphazy, Ken Rigby, Katerina Rigogiannis (who, at age five, told me how she 'blocked' a bully and helped other kids, which inspired the title of this edition), Kalman Rubin, Maree Stanley, Sonia Smith, Slater and Gordon, Maureen Stewart, Mary Tobin, Dr Mark Williams, Terry Willessee, Louise Zaetta, Sam Horn and the Maui Writers Conference, and those people in the media who have supported me from the beginning.

Many people were kind enough to tell me their stories, some of which have been included in my book, such as Ian Collet, Dallas Edwards and Allan Levy. My cousin,

Tamara Ruben, inspired me to develop the 'handpower' exercise, a key concept of this book.

Finally, I would like to thank the publisher of the Australasian edition of this book, Rex Finch, who believed in my work from the very beginning, Kathryn Lamberton, Andrew Bell, and my editor, Sean Doyle, who helped me complete this new manuscript. Together, we have created a self-help book that can be used by everyone around the world. Both Sean and Rex have inspired me to integrate my inner wisdom with my professional knowledge.

A personal message

My first book, *Bullybusting*, was influenced by my extensive personal experience as one who had been bullied at school. Since then, I have changed my perceptions about bullying. What has changed?

First, due to a blind spot of mine, I was bullied by colleagues! Clearly, the universe wanted me to add another dimension to my counselling, speaking and writing by catapulting me into a new area: workplace bullying. Since then, I have discovered that most people are capable of bullying or of being bullied, or both. Although school bullying is significantly different to workplace bullying, there are similarities. I have cross-fertilised this information and used it in this book. I know that schools are ethically responsible for stopping bullying, but I also realise that human nature will always sabotage them. As my grandmother died in a Nazi concentration camp, I believe that we need to empower children to protect themselves from mean, nasty people wherever they are.

Secondly, as a result of the bullying and what it signified to me, an old trauma was reactivated, and consequently my blood cells began bullying each other. I was quite ill for a few years, and couldn't think clearly. I rediscovered what it was like to feel stuck and powerless.

Thirdly, in doing research for a chapter in the book *Bullying Solutions*, I discovered that – despite advances in theory and in school practices – there is limited material available on the vital role that parents play in developing the crucial skills to assist targets and bullies.

Fourthly, in the intervening years – ably assisted by my video camera – I have polished my clinical practices, absorbed wonderful feedback from families, and utilised the encouraging responses to my presentations in Australia and overseas. Thus I have refined the essentials of the 'Six Secrets of Relating'.

In 2005 I attended the Maui Writers Retreat with Sam Horn. My writing was re-invigorated. The time came to update and simplify this book. *Bully Blocking* has more basic, refined, effective and practical techniques than its predecessor, and anyone can use them. This new title reflects recent changes in thinking about the bully–target 'game'. It is a prototype for all concerned: the school and its wider community, parents and students. I have brought to this revised edition a greater understanding of the role of parents, and I provide more assistance for those with bullying behaviours. This means that a child can block bullies without hurting or aggravating them, thereby leaving the door open to build respect. Similarly, bullies can 'block' their own behaviours, and schools and parents can enable children, not disable them. Implicitly, there is also a strong emphasis on skills that block bullying, regardless of what schools may be doing. These skills are well worth learning: they will protect children later on and build resilience in adulthood.

Evelyn M. Field, FAPS, ASM

Resources

School surveys

- *Peer Relations Assessment Questionnaire*, Ken Rigby, Australia

- *NCAB Do-It-Yourself Student Bullying Surveys*, National Coalition Against Bullying, Australia

- *Life in School Checklist*, Tiny Arora, UK

- *Revised Olveus Bully/Victim Questionnaire*, Dan Olveus, Norway

School programmes

- *P.E.A.C.E. Pack*, Philip Slee, Flinders University, Adelaide

- *BOUNCE BACK! Classroom Resilience Programme*, Helen McGrath & T. Noble, Pearson Education, Sydney

- *Friendly School, Friendly Families Programme*, Donna Cross, Western Australia

- *The Bullying Prevention Programme*, Dan Olveus (University of Bergen, Norway) and Susan Limber (Clemson University, US)

- *DFE Sheffield Bullying Project*, P. Smith and S. Sharp, UK

- *The Anti-Bullying Intervention in Toronto Schools*, Pepler et al., Canada

- *Peaceful Schools Project*, Dr Stuart Twemlow, Menninger Clinic, US

Websites
Use with discretion

www.bullyonline.org
www.kidscape.org.uk
www.kickbully.com
www.safechild.org
www.stopbullyingnow.com
www.bullies2buddies.com
www.kidpower.org
www.abc.tcd.ie
www.stopbullying.com
www.bullying.co.uk
www.stopbullyingme.ab.ca
www.bullying.org
www.antibully.org.uk
www.antibullying.net
www.bullypolice.org

Further reading
For parents

Besag, Valerie, *Understanding Girls' Friendships, Fights and Feuds: A practical approach to girls' bullying*, Open University Press, Philadelphia, 2006

Cohen-Posey, Kate, *How to Handle Bullies, Teasers and Other Meanies*, Rainbow Books, Highland City, Florida, 1995

Coloroso, Barbara, *The Bully, the Bullied and the Bystander*, Harper/Quill, New York, 2003

Elliot, M., *101 Ways to Deal with Bullying: A guide for parents*, Stoughton, 1997

Fried, Suellen and Fried, Paula, *Bullies and Victims: Helping your child through the schoolyard battlefield*, M. Evans and Co., New York, 1998

Griffiths, Coosje, *What Can You Do About Bullying? A guide for parents*, Meerilinga Young Children's Foundation, Perth, 1997

Grunsell, Angela, *Let's Talk About Bullying*, Alladin Books, London, 1989

Horn, Sam, *Take the Bully by the Horns: Stop unethical, uncooperative, or unpleasant people from running and ruining your life*, St. Martin's Press, New York, 2003

Jackson, Nancy F. et al., *Getting Along with Others: Teaching social effectiveness to children*, Research Press, Illinois, 1983

McCoy, Elin, *What to Do…When Kids Are Mean to Your Child*, Readers Digest, Pleasantville, New York, 1997

Mellor, Andrew, *Bullying and How to Fight It: A guide for families*, Scottish Council for Research in Education, Scotland, 1993

Pearce, Dr John, *Fighting, Teasing and Bullying*, Thorsons, London, 1989

Seddon, Cindi, McLellan, Alyson and Lajoie, Gesele, *Take Action Against Bullying*, Bully B'ware Productions, Canada, 2005

Simmons, Rachel, *Odd Girl Out: The hidden culture of aggression in girls*, Harcourt, San Diego, 2002

Sones Fineberg, Linda, *Teasing: Innocent fun or sadistic malice?*, New Horizon Press, New Jersey, 1996

Wiseman, Rosalind, *Queen Bees & Wannabes: Helping your daughter survive cliques, gossip, boyfriends & other realities of adolescence*, Random House, New York, 2002

For teachers and schools

Beane, Allan L., *Bully-Free Classroom: Over 100 tips and strategies for teachers K–8*, Free Spirit Publishing, Minneapolis, 1999

Besag, Valerie E., *Bullies and Victims in Schools*, Open University Press, Philadelphia, 1989

Garrity, Carla et al., *Bully-proofing Your School*, Sopris, West Colorado, 1997

Horne, Arthur M., Bartolomucci, Christi L., and Newman-Carlson, Dawn, *Bully Busters Grades K–5 and Grade 6–8: A teacher's manual for helping bullies, victims, and bystanders*, Research Press, Illinois, 2003

McGrath, H. and Noble, T. (eds), *Bullying Solutions*, Pearson Education, Sydney, 2005

Olveus, Dan, *Bullying at School: What we know and what we can do*, Blackwell, Oxford, 1994

O'Moore, Mona and Minton, Stephen James, *Dealing with Bullying in Schools: A training manual for teachers, parents and other professionals*, Paul Chapman, London, 2004

Randall, Peter, *Adult Bullying: Perpetrators and victims*, Routledge, London, 1997

Rigby, Ken, *Bullying in Schools and What to do About it*, ACER, Melbourne, 1996

Rigby, Ken, *Stop the Bullying: A handbook for schools*, ACER, Melbourne, 2003

Sharp, Sonia, *Reducing School Bullying – What Works?*, Institute of Education, University of Warwick, Coventry, 1997

Sharp, Sonia and Smith, Peter K. (eds), *Tackling Bullying in Your School: A practical handbook for teachers*, University of Sheffield, England, 1994

Smith, Peter K. and Sharp, Sonia (eds), *School Bullying: Insights and perspectives*, University of Sheffield, England, 1994

Sullivan, K., *Bullying: How to Spot It and How to Stop It – A guide for parents and teachers*, Rodale International, New York, 2006

Sullivan, Keith, *The Anti-Bullying Handbook*, Oxford UP, New Zealand, 2000

Sullivan, Keith, Cleary, Mark and Sullivan, Ginny, *Bullying in Secondary Schools: What it looks like and how to manage it*, Paul Chapman, London, 2004

Evelyn M. Field is available to give public and school presentations. For further information, either email Evelyn at info@bullying.com.au or visit her website: www.bullying.com.au.

Index

abusive behaviours 136–7
  see also bullying; sexual harassment
academic effects of bullying 33–4,
    49–50, 55
action talk 197–8
'Activate your power' exercise 70–71
adolescence 155–7
adulthood, difficulties in 54–5, 56, 77,
    109
aggression 18–19, 134, 135–6
anchors, use of 71–2
anger 66, 143–4, 151
anti-bullying strategies, schools 39–40,
    110–25
anxiety, dealing with 144–5
appearance 183–4
assertive behaviour 135–6
assertive language 193–200
attention, negative 23–4, 27, 152
attention-seeking behaviours 94
attitudes, changing 59–66, 67–75
  see also confidence
avoidance ideas 96–7, 233

bad habits, getting rid of 65–6
'Be a fun person' exercise 172
beliefs, faulty 63–5
belly-button watcher ('BBW') 65–6,
    175
biochemical treatment 140
blank face 188
blank-out moments 196

boarding schools 106
body chart 145
body language *see* nonverbal
    communication
body movements 189–90, 191
'Bossing your inner bully' exercise 169
boys
  bullying tactics 21, 30
  communication skills 195
  development rates 156
  peer-group relationships 157
  socialising 154–5
breathing 193
bribery 88
bullies
  characteristics of 21–2, 24, 27–8,
    29–31
  effects on 60
  feelings of 132
  healthy lifestyles 89
  home bullies 79–80
  identifying 234
  kids' comments on 15
  need for reaction 23–4
  parenting 92–3, 97
  parents of 45, 161–2
  relationship with target 23
  responses to retorts 214–15
  teachers responses to 234–5
bullying
  behaviours 28, 136–7
  causes 29, 37–46

bullying *cont.*
    effects 33–4, 49–56, 132, 133–4,
      165
    facts about 16–17
    identifying 80–84, 234
    management of incidents 119–21
    predictability of 159–62
    rules of the game 21–6
    understanding why 148–63
    warning signs 33–4
    see also physical bullying; property
      bullying; social bullying; teasing
bullying paradox 38
butterfly symbol 128
bystanders *see* witnesses

careers, effects of bullying 55
change
    after therapy 76, 125
    in bully behaviours 137
    of direction 68
    practising 88
chatting 224
children *see* adolescence; only children
collaborative school strategy 111
comebacks *see* retorts
comfort check 142
communication skills
    benefits of 180–81
    checklist 181
    gender differences 195
    practice techniques 184–5
    see also nonverbal communication;
      verbal power skills
computers, effects 43–4, 90, 218
confidence-booster list 169
confidence building 86–7, 165–6, 169,
    182–3, 217
confrontation 123, 140–41
connecting statements 196, 198
cool, looking 183–4
coping mechanisms 96–7
copy-cat behaviour 182–3, 191
counselling 102–4, 123–5
crisis management, schools 119–21
criticism *see* families, criticism of;
    feedback; teasing
cultural differences 37, 38, 153–5

culture, of schools 111, 162
cyber bullying 44, 90, 218

'Decorate the mirror' exercise 171
democratic families 41
depression 54
differences
    accepting 60, 62
    cultural 37, 38, 153–5
    negotiating 225
    see also 'special' children
disabilities 102, 150
discipline 41, 122–3
'Do I belong?' dilemma 157
doing nothing 38–9, 66, 152, 218
drugs, for releasing feelings 140

educational programmes 113–14,
    115–16, 235–6
    see also training programmes
electronic 'blah blah' 43–4, 90
emotional effects of bullying 34, 52–4,
    55
    see also feelings
empathy 78, 80, 225
empowerment 168, 173
environmental factors 153–5
ethical obligations of schools 109–110
evaluation
    of anti-bullying strategies 125
    of progress 97–8
exclusion 18–19, 34, 220–22
extended families, break-up of 42–3
'eye talk' 185–7, 217

face talk 187–9
fairness, lack of 63–4
faking confidence 166, 171
families
    criticism of 62–3
    effect of bullying 55
    influence on behaviour 78–80
    role of 41–4
    secrets 86, 158–9
    structures 42–3, 159–62
    table talk 199–200
    time together 85

fear, not showing 66
feedback
  from bullies 174
  from teachers 175
  negative 152, 173–4, 176
  positive 173–4, 175, 178–9
  'shopping' exercise 176
  types of 73
  using 72–3, 173–6, 198, 226
'"Feelgood" list' exercise 171
feelings
  expression of 134–7
  identifying 137–9
  listing exercise 133–4, 145
  major 133
  parents' 77–8
  regulating 131–2
  releasing 139–47
  see also emotional effects
'fight or flight' mode 53, 67, 131
fighting back 94, 218
'Finger exercise for jigglers' 186–7
first impressions 182
fitness 217
fitting in 182–4
'fowl that plays foul' bullies 30–31
friendships
  building 197–8, 224–7, 230, 231
  changing 25–6, 27
  characteristics 225–6, 231
  variety in 226
  see also support networks

gender see boys; girls
genetic factors 150–53
genograms 159–62
girls
  bullying tactics 21
  communication skills 195
  development rates 156
  peer-group relationships 157
  socialising 154–5
giving
  to others 176–7
  to yourself 168–72
grandparents 45, 162
group action, by parents 100–101
group identity 18–19, 23–4, 38, 40,
    152, 182–4

see also difference; peer groups
'gut-talk' 196–7, 198–9

'Handpower' exercise 215–16
happy, looking 146
harassment 20–21
headteachers, role of 40
healthy lifestyle 89, 217
'hear no evil' 39
helplessness 54, 64–5
home bullies 79–80
home schooling 106
hormones, stress-related 131
hot spots, avoiding 233
'How do you look?' checklist 184
humour
  use of 90–91
  see also retorts

'I' statements 196–7, 198–9
independence 63
'Instant confidence' exercise 182
intellectual see academic
interest, showing 224–5
investigation of bullying, in schools
    112–13
isolated targets 24–5

justice, belief in 63–4

law of averages 69, 89
learning difficulties 150
learning styles 116
legal obligations of schools 109–110
legal options 101, 121
lone parents 42, 43, 161
loser behaviours 136

malicious bullies 29–30, 234
media action 101–2
medication 140
mentoring 115
mindset see attitudes
'Misery tree' exercise 158
mood flips 68–9
moving
  countries 154–5
  schools 104–5

negative attention 23–4, 27, 152
negative feedback 152, 173–4, 176
no-blame approach 121
non-bullying interaction 25–6
non-malicious bullies 30–31, 234
nonverbal communication 185–92
normal, need to be 153

older parents 44
only children 41, 224
overprotection 41, 42, 44, 86, 92, 97,
    102, 159

pain, fear of 65
parenting
    of bullies 92–3, 97
    guidelines 92
    reduced time for 43
    and self-esteem 177–9
parents
    action plan 94–9
    of bullies 45
    group action 100–101
    identifying bullying 80–84
    older 44
    own feelings 77–8
    with problems 42, 45, 78
    referral concerns 103–4
    as role models 78–9
    and schools 40, 98–101
    as social coaches 84–5, 92–3
    of targets 45, 160–61
    training programs for 117–18
passive-aggressive behaviour 134
passive behaviour 134, 135–6
'Past and present teases' exercise 203
peer groups 25–6, 40, 55–6, 157
    see also difference; group identity
peer mediation 120
pep-talks 170, 171
personal space 191–2
personality, role of 150–51
pets 178
physical bullying 19–20, 49, 219–20
physical environment, improving
    118–19
physical release of feelings 141–2
physical signs of bullying 33
positive behaviours 137, 146

positive feedback 173–4, 175, 178–9
power
    taking back 67–72, 215–16
    use, abuse or lose 134–7
    of witnesses 25, 236
power tools 222
prince/princess-in-training 43, 160
principals, role of 40
progress, assessing 97–8
property bullying 219–20
provocation 94, 152
psychological effects of bullying 52–4,
    55
psychological support see counselling
public relations, in schools 113
pupils see students

quick fixes for feelings release 143
'Quiet voice' exercise 194

reactive targets 44–5
record keeping 80–83, 96, 113, 217
relationships 23, 54–5, 228
    see also friendships; group identity;
        peer groups; social skills
relocation see moving
reporting bullying 95, 112, 115, 119,
    123, 236
resilience training 87
restorative practices 121
results, slow 64, 68, 89
retaliatory behaviours 94, 218
retorts 91, 204, 206–215, 236
rewards 68, 88, 178, 185, 188
role models 78–9, 86

sabotaging efforts 97
sadness, dealing with 145
safety 94, 141, 205
'saltwater crocodile' bullies 29–30
sanctions for bullying 122–3
school phobia/refusal 54
schools
    anti-bullying strategies 39–40,
        110–25
    culture 111, 162
    effects of bullying 55
    moving 104–6

obligations 108–110
and parents 40, 98–101
role of 38–40, 98–9
see also principals; staff; teachers
secrets, family 86, 158–9
'see no evil' 38–9
self-acceptance 63, 167
self-blame 60–61
self-esteem 52, 55, 151, 164–79
self-esteem bank 167, 168
self-identity 156–7
sensitivities, heightened 61–2, 150–51
sexual harassment 20–21, 218
sexuality, developing 156
shared concern method 120–21
'Shopping' exercise, on feedback 176
'Shopping list' (self-esteem) 165–6
shyness 35, 54, 76, 153
siblings 41
single parents 42, 43, 161
smiles 74, 187–8
social bullying 18–19, 34, 220–22
social coaching *see* social skills
social effects of bullying 50–51, 55
social phobia 54
social signs of bullying 34
social skills
benefits of 224–5
developing 84–8, 92–3, 115–16,
224–9
gender differences 154–5
guidelines 25–6
problems with 152–3
score sheet 228–9
see also friendships; relationships
'speak no evil' 39
speaking skills 193–4
'special' children 159
see also difference; disabilities;
overprotection
staff
training programmes for 116–17
see also headteachers; teachers
stress, dealing with 144–5
'strip the tease' guidelines 203–4
students
educational programmes for
113–14, 115–16, 235–6
see also bullies; peer groups; targets
'Success stories' exercise 170

suicidal tendencies 54
support networks
benefits of 63, 224–5
creating 25, 78
identification exercise 232
in schools 111
see also friendships
survival instinct 53, 67
swearing 83, 202–3

table talk 199–200
'Take a chance' exercise 70
talented, being 150
targets
becoming 32
characteristics 44–5
consequences for 48–54
healthy lifestyles 89, 217
as home bullies 79–80
identifying 31–2, 80–84, 234
isolated 24–5
reactions of 23–4
reactive 44–5
relationship with bully 23
shy child checklist 35
teachers' responses to 235
understanding why 148–63
task forces, in schools 111–12
tea bag trick 190
teachers
bullying of 109
effects of bullying 55
feedback from 175
issues for 234–6
see also staff
teasing
dealing with 24, 203–214
listing exercise 203
main types 17–18, 202–3
response checklist 205–6
'That's not me!' 166
'Three Monkeys' attitude 38–9
training programmes, in schools
114–18
truth, about self 62

verbal bullying *see* teasing
verbal power skills 140–41, 193–200
see also retorts

victims *see* targets
visualisation 172, 190–91, 193
voice power 193–4

warning signs 33–4
'Who am I' dilemma 156–7
'Whodunnit' exercise 80–83
whole-school policy 110–111
witnesses 25, 39, 55–6, 115, 236
workplace bullying 56, 77, 109
workplace skills 85–6
wrong time and place 149